SERMONS TO THE NOVICES REGULAR

THOMAS A KEMPIS

AETERNA PRESS

PUBLISHED BY AETERNA PRESS.
COVER DESIGN BY AETERNA PRESS.

THOMAS À KEMPIS CANON REGULAR OF THE CONGREGATION OF WINDESHEIM

AUTHORISED TRANSLATION FROM THE TEXT OF THE EDITION OF MICHAEL JOSEPH POHL, PH.D.

BY DOM VINCENT SCULLY, C.R.L. (PERMISSU SUPERIORUM)

LONDON KEGAN PAUL, TRENCH, TRÜBNER & CO., LTD. DRYDEN HOUSE, GERRARD STREET, W.
1907

TO THE PROFESSED NOVICES OF THE ENGLISH PROVINCE OF THE CANONS REGULAR OF THE LATERAN

ISBN-13: 978-1-78516-107-0

AVAILABLE AS AN E-BOOK:
WWW.AETERNAPRESS.COM

CONTENTS

INTRODUCTION

FOR many years the Venerable Thomas à Kempis had charge of the young Religious at Mount St. Agnes. The office of training the Novices was with the Windesheimers usually attached to the sub-priorship, at least in the early days of the Congregation, and a Novice-Master, as such, was not appointed. Twice Thomas was elected Sub-Prior of the Monastery on the Mount. We find him named as holding that post in 1429, in a list of the Brethren who went into exile rather than disobey a papal interdict laid upon the land. As a vacancy had occurred by the promotion of Brother Theodoric from Sub-Prior to Prior in 1425, it is reasonable to presume that our author was appointed at that date.

During the period of exile in Frisia, three years or longer, the community would be more or less disorganized; moreover, during part of that time Thomas was posted by his superiors at Arnheim to aid his brother John à Kempis, who was failing in health and who died in 1432, assisted by Thomas to the end. Meanwhile another had been elected Sub-Prior of Mount St. Agnes. But in 1448 we find our Venerable Thomas chosen Sub-Prior again, and this time he seems to have remained in office for a long period: the next Sub-Prior mentioned is Henry Ruhorst, whose death is chronicled in 1458.

The fact of our author's close relations as Sub-Prior with the younger members of the Community explains not only the present volume of sermons, but also the great proportion among his writings of treatises intended chiefly for youthful Religious, as "The Discipline of the Cloister," "The Monk's Alphabet," "The Manual for Beginners," etc. "He composed various treatises for the edification of youth, unadorned and simple in style, but truly great in thought and efficacy," says the unknown continuator of the "Chronicles of Mount St. Agnes," in his necrology notice of our Venerable Thomas. And he adds, "he possessed a wonderful gift of consoling the tempted and afflicted."

In fact, tradition represents him to us as particularly skilled in the direction of souls, a gift it is not difficult to concede to the author of the "Imitation," and as especially happy and successful in the encouragement and instruction of the young. "There is an interesting picture given of him," writes Kettlewell, "which is said to have been taken from an engraving on copper, found over his grave when his bones were dug up in the burial ground of Mount St. Agnes. In this picture Thomas à Kempis is represented as coming forward on the elevated part of the chancel to receive a young man anxiously desirous to forsake the world and its vanities, and to enter upon a religious state. The young man is seen approaching the reverend Father, reverently bowing his knee, and saying:

'O where is peace? For thou its path hast trod.'

This is on a scroll which he bears in his hand; and Thomas à Kempis gives the following reply on another scroll which he carries:

'In poverty, retirement, and with God.' "

This answer is certainly characteristic, as a perusal of the present volume will abundantly show.

The Windesheimers were exceedingly careful, as might be expected, in the reception and subsequent training of candidates for the Religious Life in the Canonical Order. One reads in their Statutes or Constitutions: "We consider that the greatest possible care and diligence should be exercised in the reception of Novices; inasmuch as the perverse and indocile, if admitted to mingle with the good, are often wont to cause serious harm to religion, and inasmuch as the good after their admission, if left without due instruction, suffer grave loss in the negligence of religion."

The Constitutions then proceed to proscribe all merely human motives in the acceptance of postulants: "For the admission therefore of all who may come and seek the religious habit, we decree that this primary care and caution be exercised, namely that neither for dignity of family nor for multitude of riches, nor for any other consideration pertaining to the pomp or avarice of this world, any be accepted, whose fellowship is known as likely to cause harm or danger or disgrace to the rest established in religion, either because of the depravity of their own conduct, or through the annoyance and importunity of others among their acquaintance or kinsfolk."

Then are added the qualifications which should be sought in the candidates: "But we counsel that you should consider in those who would be received, in the first place good conduct, and especially that they be meek and tractable and not impatient of correction."

Further precautions are then taken to secure that no candidate be admitted even to the Noviciate hastily or without full deliberation: "Unknown persons who do not bring with them trustworthy testimonials we do not admit before the probation of half a year, unless the Community unanimously, or at least three parts of the Community, judge that a less lengthy delay may be accorded.

"During this period they should be tried whether they be constant in their purpose, and perfectly renounce the pomps of the world by the casting aside of worldly garments, by the exercise of toil and humiliation, by ready submission to all commands and hardships, by mortification of their own will and opinion, by observance of silence and quiet, by zeal in sacred reading and prayer, by the grateful acceptance of blame and correction, by cheerfulness in the watchings and fasts, by readiness to confess their sins, and to disclose their temptations, and all other the like wherein they can be proved, whether they truly will to die to the world and themselves and live to God in the perfection of holy Religion."

Excluded from admission were: (1) Youths under eighteen; after the Council of Trent, the age limit was sixteen. (2) A Cleric or Lay-Brother from another Monastery, except by leave of the General Chapter. (3) Two brothers, or father and son, in the same house, except again by permission of the General Chapter; in this case the second comer was not to have a voice in the Chapter, except by dispensation. (4) Secular priests, or those of illegitimate birth.

In accordance with papal decrees, no gift of any kind, under any pretext whatever, was to be demanded of the postulants.

If, finally, a candidate was accepted as such, he was to be very fully instructed in the obligations, burdens, and difficulties of the Religious Life, and in the Rule and Statutes of the Order; if this severe presentment did not dismay him he was to be further initiated into the choir duties of reading and chant. Then, on an appointed day he was led into the Chapter Room, where, duly instructed beforehand, he prostrated himself at the Prior's feet.

"What is your request?" the Prior asked.

"I beg God's mercy and your fellowship," was the reply.

Then rising to his knees at the command of the Prior, he is questioned by him before the whole assembly: whether he had come from another Order: whether he was free: whether he had plighted his troth to any woman: whether he was bound by any vow: whether he suffered from any hidden and incurable disease: whether he was involved in any quarrel or debt: whether born in lawful wedlock: whether he was capable of receiving Holy Orders.

After receiving a satisfactory answer to all these various questions, the Prior again insisted on the difficulties and hardships of the Religious Life, especially such as were entailed in the renunciation of self-will and constant obedience, warning him at the same time with what unsparing severity a strict observance of every point of religious discipline would be exacted, and how sternly every defect would be punished. The candidate is then asked whether he still perseveres in his request.

"Then if undismayed and constant he reply, that trusting solely in the loving-kindness of God and the prayers of the Brethren, he will accomplish all these things, the Prior shall say: 'May the Lord grant thee to fulfill all this, that thou mayest attain eternal life.' "

Taking the kneeling postulant's hands in his own, the Prior proceeds: "On the part of God and our own, we grant thee our fellowship."

He would add that the postulant was fully free to depart before his profession, as it was also always in the power of the Order to dismiss him before that act, should he prove an unsuitable subject: and finally a day was assigned him for his clothing in the religious habit.

For this solemn investiture, which was to mark the commencement of his Noviciate proper, the postulant was instructed to prepare himself by a General Confession and Holy Communion. The clothing took place in the Sacristy, between the recitation of the Office and the Conventual Mass: the tyro was divested of his upper garment and robed in the white cassock and linen rochet of the Order. He was then led to the High Altar and lay prostrate there during the singing of the "Veni Creator" and the customary versicles and collects. Finally, he was received to the kiss of peace by the Prior and the assembled Brethren.

The Novice's rochet, then as now, was distinguished from that of a professed Canon by short sleeves, in place of the long, to signify his freedom as yet from the vows. He was also not permitted to wear the amess, an article of dress which survives to-day in the cape of the Secular Canon.

The Novice was now entrusted to a Brother "of good repute," in the early years of the Congregation usually the Sub-Prior, to be diligently instructed even in the minutest details of the Regular Life, "as to his carriage, his bearing, his every gesture, how to keep his eyes cast down, to speak modestly and not hastily, and in all his movements to give proof of humility." He was also to be taught how to read and chant in the different tones, according to the diversity of the season; and it was the special duty of the Novice to sing the versicles on his side of the choir.

"He shall also be taught how to address the Prior and the Brethren, and that he must especially show reverence to the Prior. And, above all, he shall be frequently admonished to change his worldly conduct and habits unto better, and to put off the old man with his deeds, confessing and punishing with tears the evil he has wrought, repressing also his vices and the concupiscence of the flesh, mortifying likewise his own will and judgement for the good of obedience, and embracing all things lowly and base, and labours of whatsoever kind, and then by pursuing virtue become a new man in Christ."

And the better to attain this, "as one dead to the world and himself, let him in no wise mingle with the external affairs or business of the house in private or public, seeking to live to God alone, a zealous guardian of his cell and quiet; let him shun growing slack in idleness, and following the counsel and instruction of his master let him set his soul to spiritual progress, being instant in holy reading and prayer, and compunction of heart and meditation, or else in labour of the hands in his cell or without, as shall be enjoined him, according to the rule of our common practice." It would be difficult to find a more exact conformity than exists between these prescriptions and the oft-repeated counsels contained in the following discourses.

And how well the following paragraph fits in with the subject matter of his Third Sermon: "And that he may the more efficaciously consult his own welfare, he should very often manifest to his master all his temptations and the secrets of his heart and his whole life, and have nothing that he would wish concealed from him or the Prior of the house."

And again, "let no man," says à Kempis, "looking at others, neglect himself: having a care of himself before all, let him be silent as to the rest, which does not concern his charge," p. 19. And the Constitutions, speaking of the Novice: "And he should not freely thrust himself into the discourse or business of others, but showing honour to all, let him hardly venture to say anything in the presence of others, and when questioned, let him learn to answer humbly and in few words, with modesty and fear."

"And to the Community gatherings, where his presence is required, especially in the Divine Office, let him accustom himself to hasten devoutly and betimes, day and night, with all alacrity and fervour of spirit." To this "alacrity and fervour of spirit," especially in the Divine Office, our Venerable Thomas encourages his Novices in his very first Sermon: and again in Sermon VI he encourages them to struggle against the very natural difficulty that must have beset many to remain wakeful through the long night vigils. In the third Example which he cites there for the edification of his young hearers, it is thought that he is referring to the holy man William Vorniken, for many years Prior of Mount St. Agnes, so well does the narrative fit in with what we learn of the character of this venerable Canon from Busch in his Chronicle of Windesheim. But for the rest it must be freely admitted that joyous devotion in the praise of God was a common characteristic of all the Devout Brothers and Canons of Windesheim, and pre-eminently of Thomas himself.

Who can read unmoved the eloquent testimony of Francis Tolensis on this point? And this writer earnestly assures us that in his brief biography he has carefully eschewed all mere rhetorical flourish and has strictly adhered to the simple truth, as found in contemporary documents, or handed down by tradition in Mount St. Agnes, of which monastery he was himself a member.

"In the Church," he writes, "and in the performance of ecclesiastical ceremonies, it is difficult to describe his rapt attention, and I might say inspiration. While he chanted the psalms, his eyes were ever raised towards Heaven, and he appeared to be filled with a divine enthusiasm, captivated and carried away by the unutterable sweetness of the holy psalmody: so that he never stood with his heels resting upon the ground; that is to say, as he meditated the tips of his toes alone touched the floor, the rest of his body was lifted heavenwards, whither his soul tended with all its desires. In the Divine Office he always remained standing erect, never sitting, never resting his arm, or leaning back against the stall. Of those that entered the choir, night or day, he was always the first; of those that left he was always the last. Incredible was his delight in and his love for the Divine worship and the services of the Church. So evident was this pleasure that one day some one remarked to Thomas that he considered him very fortunate, and after all not so much deserving of praise in the alacrity of his voice, the joyousness of his soul, and his piety in singing the psalms, because those psalms were as sweet to him as salmon. 'Thanks be to God,' Thomas replied, 'the psalms are indeed to me as salmon; nevertheless their taste is frequently turned to bitterness and death, when I perceive any idly inattentive to the matter in hand, or sparing their voice.' "

Finally, the Master of the Novice is bidden "often to consider his daily life, and whether he does anything in excess or in default of what is befitting, in order to correct him in secret and instruct him as may be necessary."

And here I will close the quotations from the Windesheim Constitutions regarding the reception and training of the Novices. Those who desire an account of the Solemn Profession, or taking of the vows, which generally followed at the end of the year's noviciate, may consult the "Life of the Venerable Thomas à Kempis," quoted above, p. 114.

Enough meanwhile has been said to enable the reader of the following Sermons to appreciate the position of à Kempis as Novice Master, and the appropriateness of the greater part of the discourses here given. For they treat precisely, as we have already partly seen, of those virtues and practices which were especially required of the young Religious, if they were to progress and persevere in their holy vocation: lessons of obedience, humility, modesty, patience, love of the cloister, of solitude and silence, zeal for the worship of God, and devotion to the angels and saints, to the holy Mother of God, and above all to the person of Jesus Christ, the whole interwoven with constant reference to the eternal rewards and punishments of the life to come.

For the rest these are favourite subjects with à Kempis, and are to be found passim throughout his works.

Usually, as befits the matter and the audience, and as the author himself says in the Preface, the style is of the simplest. But there is always to be remarked that easy flow of language together with that precision of expression, which are familiar to à Kempis scholars, but for which the venerable Thomas has not yet received sufficient general recognition: at times indeed, as for instance in Sermon XVI, he rises to heights of real eloquence, not unworthy of the great St. Augustine, whose works he so closely studied.

Moreover it should be noted that although these discourses are addressed directly to Novices and adapted chiefly to their needs, they are animated with the same spirit, they vibrate and palpitate with the same life as the other works of the Venerable Author, and especially his masterpiece, the "Imitation," the spirit namely and the life of the Mystics of Windesheim. The essence of this mysticism, as of all true mysticism, is union of the soul with God. The first step towards this union is the removal of all obstacles in the way. The first hindrance is sin: hence the need not only of the abandonment of sin now in the thorough conversion of the soul and all its faculties to God, but of constant further purification by continual grief and penance for past guilt. Then must follow the removal of all other impediments induced by the soul's undue attachment to self and creatures, and this by mortification in every shape and form, exterior and interior, by obedience, humility, patience, poverty, chastity. And yet all this is only so much preparatory spade-work, the degree and the perfection of the actual union itself, the realization of the mystic state, are in proportion only to the actual Love of the soul for its Creator, a Love nurtured first by sensible affections and intense personal devotion to the God-Man, Christ, but ascending finally to a simple, indescribable resting and breathing of the soul in the contemplation of the pure, indivisible Essence of the Godhead.

The reader will notice and doubtless smile at the simplicity of the reason given by the author in the Prologue for his division of the Sermons into three parts, containing respectively nine, ten, and eleven discourses. But any one acquainted with the writings of the early Fathers knows how fondly they dwelt on the figurative symbolism of numbers: and saturated, so to speak, as they were, with these writings, it is but natural that the Windesheimers should have acquired something of the same habit. In explanation of the rather obscure passage, regarding the Third Part that "it contains eleven Sermons to designate the religious state, in the renouncing of the world and carrying of the cross," I venture to suggest that eleven is taken as typical of the Cloister, because it consists of ten, the number of the Decalogue, plus one, the counsel of perfection embraced in Religion.

Before concluding I must refer to the extraordinary statement of the Rev. S. Kettlewell that "there is some question, however, as to whether he (à Kempis) ever wrote the third part or series of the 'Sermons to the Novices.' The subjects are wholly different from the first two series, and relate more to the corruptions and superstitions of the Church before the Reformation era. But supposing those sermons in the third series were his, it is questionable whether he would have suffered them to have been published, had he been alive. Of all those treatises which are found re-written by his own hand, we may presume that he gave his sanction to their being made public. But of the others there is reason to doubt whether he would have wished them to have gone forth at all, or not without some correction at least."

Of course, the sole reason for the position here assumed by Mr. Kettlewell is found in the second sentence quoted above. The same unhappy prejudice explains much that mars his otherwise excellent work. But I am convinced that even he could never have penned these words, if he had been privileged, as I was, to see and handle the autograph volume of à Kempis, containing these Sermons, bound with the Life of Lydwine, Virgin, now preserved in the University Library, Louvain.

Dr. Pohl's text, of which the following pages are an exact rendering, is a very painstaking edition of this precious original.

THE TRANSLATOR.

ST. IVES, CORNWALL.

Feast of St. Joseph, 1907.

PROLOGUE OF THE SERMONS TO THE NOVICES REGULAR

TO the beloved brethren in Christ, Innocent, Simplician and the other followers of the Crucified, who love the discipline of holy religion: a Brother Pilgrim dwelling in the vale of tears: humbly seeking the aid of your prayers. May the peace of Christ abound in your hearts: and may manifold patience be vouchsafed to you and to me in the Cross of Christ. The Sermons, which although given to our Novices by way of sweet conference at different times, I have gathered into one: I have thought good, and deemed just to communicate in charity to you. Albeit, therefore, the discourse be uncouth and the matter not subtle: nevertheless, wishing to please simple minds, that which the Lord has inspired and bestowed: I freely offer to the pious and devout to read. But if haply an ill-chosen word offend any one, I pray that my littleness be forgiven: and that what seems outwardly to sound ridiculous, be changed to something better. And because examples often move one's hearers more than words alone: therefore taught by the custom of blessed Gregory, in several places at the end of the sermon for greater insistence I have briefly noted certain examples, as they came to mind. Receive graciously, Brothers, what I offer to you as to dear friends: pray that it may be all to the honour of God and the profit of many.

The Sermons of the First Part of this Book

The Sermons of the Second Part

The Sermons of the Third Part

The End of the Chapters

This Book contains thirty sermons, and it has three Parts. The First Part contains nine sermons, to designate the nine choirs of the angels. The Second Part contains ten sermons, to designate the decalogue of the law, according to the number of the ten commandments. The Third Part contains eleven sermons, to designate the religious state, in the renouncing of the world and carrying of the Cross, according to the counsel of our Saviour saying: "If any man will come after Me, let him deny himself, and take up his cross and follow Me."

SERMONS TO THE NOVICES

PART I

SERMON I

OF THE CONCORD OF BRETHREN AND THE MELODY OF DIVINE PRAISE

BEHOLD how good and how pleasant it is: for brethren to dwell together in unity. David, a saint and a truly great prophet before God, filled with the Holy Ghost, composed many psalms: some for the seeking of aid in tribulation, others in thanksgiving for deliverance from enemies. But seldom or never did he produce so good and so pleasant a melody as he uttered in this short gradual canticle, saying: Behold how good and how pleasant it is for brethren to dwell together in unity. For all naturally seek good and pleasantness: but flee from evil and sadness, as man's unhappiness. Therefore eager to speak of brotherly love and concord, passing over in silence other present goods he rejoiced especially in the devotion of brethren: and taking up his pleasant psaltery with the harp he sang in the house of the Lord saying: Behold how good and how pleasant it is: for brethren to dwell together in unity. Truly, Brethren, there is no greater happiness in a monastery of religious and a community of Brothers and Sisters: than unanimity of soul, and concord in virtue with observance of the rule and statutes: according to the precepts of superiors, and the counsel of elders. But this holy and God-pleasing concord of brethren the devil, the enemy of all the good, ceases not to combat and assault: in divers ways day and night laying snares to beguile slothful and unwary souls: and at one time indeed he troubles openly by vain speeches: at another he tempts and unsettles by vile suggestions: thereby to draw away the few soldier of Christ from his holy purpose: or to bring the veteran follower into slothfulness; or to urge the weak into murmuring: or to bind the passionate in obstinacy. But against these wiles and terrors of Satan a united community of brethren struggles and triumphs; who watch in vigils by night, toil in labours by day: give heed to sacred reading; instant in devout prayers and the melody of psalms sing praise to God: and as it were trumpeting together on heavenly bugles put the demon to flight. For they torment him mightily when they fast, they strike him when they take the discipline: they tread him under foot when they beg pardon, they crush him when they humble themselves; they terrify him when they call on Jesus, they torture him when they name Mary: they drive him away when they sign themselves with the cross, they burn him when they worship the Crucified; they conquer when they obey, they straiten when they abide in solitude: they bind when they keep strict silence. Truly this is the holy assembly of the brethren who seek the Lord; who seek the face of the God of Jacob: who spurn the world, love Christ, renounce themselves and all things for God's sake; fight against the devil and his host until he retires: and is afraid to return again soon to the camp of God. Weigh therefore, most beloved, how good it is and sweet for brethren to dwell together in unity; who gathered in one house, bound together by the profession of one rule, well ordered under one superior, rise together to the watches, come together to the canonical Hours, begin together to chant and read: strive together to perform the Divine Office worthily. Oh how pleasing and praiseworthy the assembly devoted chiefly to the praise of God; where there are as many resounding trumpets: as there are voices cheerfully singing in choir.

But hearing this, what say the demons who trouble religious? us flee from Israel," they say, "this holy and devout community: for the Lord fighteth with them against us. These are the true Israelites who, going forth from Egypt and the darkness of a worldly life, for Christ's sake have left relatives and friends; and now clothed in the habit of holy religion, have vowed themselves to God for ever and have commenced bravely to fight against us: certainly to our confusion and to the increase of their glory." Stand with constancy therefore, brethren, armed by prayers against the foes of your salvation, fearing the onslaught of none: but trusting in the Lord give thanks for all the blessings bestowed upon you, in preference to many wandering in the world. Grow not weary of rising every night to the nocturnal watches; but when the signal is given, throw off sleepiness from your eyes, distractions from your hearts: dissoluteness from your conduct. Ah, dearly beloved, give heed to the presence of Christ, the guard of angels, the reverence due to the Sacrament and the relics of the saints; in whose sight you stand and sing psalms: although with bodily eyes you see them not. Beware carefully of vain imaginations and unclean spirits: lest they find room to enter and lie hid in you. Swiftly turn away your face from the traffic of the devil: sign your hearts with the sign of the holy cross: flee to the Passion of Christ: blush to think on other things than the words of God which you read and chant. Begin now to lead a celibate life with the angels; keep peace and concord with all: give occasion of scandal to none by words or offensive actions. In the charity of Christ bear with the shortcomings of the weak: be not, however, in agreement with their bad habits or complaints. Pray often for the tried and the tempted: fear lest the like befall you, or you incur worse. And to all show an example of true humility, mildness, patience, silence and obedience: that you may receive an everlasting reward from God with His saints and elect in Heaven. For if you knew their least joy: you would fly to all the things that please God: and would hasten to the choir where things divine and heavenly are discoursed day and night. When, therefore, you feel weariness of heart from the burden of the toil: remember the eternal rewards promised you in Heaven. Whence blessed Paul, who toiled more than all, arousing the slothful, strengthening the weak: amid his labours recalled the things of Heaven to mind saying. "The sufferings of this time are not worthy to be compared: with the glory to come, that shall be revealed in us." Never shall the servant of God possibly be overcome in the combat, or weighed down by the toil of time: who always bears in mind eternal goods or evils. Who therefore wishes to have a heart pure and quiet, let him shut out from himself all earthly ease and human solace. For speedily is lost the desire of Heaven acquired in silence: unless it be guarded with all diligence from rumours from without.

A convent of monks is like the salt sea, which cannot retain within it dead bodies: but at once casts up on the shore what is corrupt, but nourishes what is healthy and fresh: and bringing it to perfection, renders it agreeable to the beholder. Know therefore that a carnal man concealed under a poor garment, cannot long disguise himself: but either in himself he falls away through lukewarmness, and dries up in his fervour; or he speedily departs, or meditates departure: or remaining with murmuring, shows of himself the corruption of perverse conduct. And because he is light of heart and unbridled of mouth, he often mocks others; because proud and passionate, he arouses strife among the peaceful, and accuses the simple. And because he has not the root of humility, and heeds not to pluck out the thorns of sensuality: therefore he is unable to produce the sweet flowers of chastity with the fruits of obedience and charity.

In a community of the Devout the hearts of many are tried, as gold in a burning furnace: whether their desires are of God, or conceived of the flesh. For who seek their own ease, and carelessly pass over community tasks and the observances of the Order; these make little progress in the spirit: but turning aside to outward things they often slip back to former evil ways. How shall anyone be able to persevere long in discipline and devotion; who does not strive manfully against temptations and passions? Wherefore, while little vices lie hid, the remedies should be applied in due time: lest the thorns growing up choke the good seed. For the Saviour says of certain feigned and lukewarm brothers, in whom there is not spiritual fervour: but only the outward humble habit is seen with the desire of honour. "Every plant which My heavenly Father hath not planted: shall be rooted up." in sooth he who does not build his house upon the strong rock, that is, his life upon Christ and true humility: when the wind of pride blows, he falls from the state of devotion to external occupations: and into divers temptations of the devil. From which evils may Jesus Christ, the Son of God, lovingly defend us: Who hath taught us by word and example to walk humbly: and ever to keep peace with the brethren without guile and dissipation. Amen.

SERMON II

OF THE PRAISE OF A GOOD CONGREGATION

BROTHER that is helped by his brother: is like a strong city. Beloved brethren, remark these words wisely and fruitfully uttered by Solomon: and keep with perseverance your places in a good community. Bear with one another in all humility and mildness, carrying your burdens: for the sake of escaping many dangers, and meriting very great rewards from God for your soul. a good Congregation: is as a tower of strength against the face of the enemy. For there a man lives with greater safety: there he is aided by many. And if at times he is troubled by one: again he is comforted by another. He who is of good will and seeks God: will make greater progress, and stand more firmly among them that seek God. There a man is more tried, and exercised in virtue: there he is frequently reproved for negligence. There he is drawn to higher perfection by word and example: there he is forced to consider and lament his own imperfection. There he is aroused by the fervour of one: he is taught by the humility of another; he is moved by the obedience of this one: he is edified by the patience of that. There he blushes to be less generous: there he is ashamed to be found less eager. There he finds some to fear; there he has some to love: and thus he profits by all. There the correction of another, is his own warning: there another's danger, is his mirror. There one is the warden of another: and one proves another in patience. There a man bears and is borne: there he hears and sees much from which he may learn. There the rule and holy custom keep in good: there confession and discipline correct excesses. There the good are commended that they may become better: there the careless are rebuked that they may grow fervent again. There a man is not suffered to become lukewarm: nor to act according to his own whim. There he is compelled to serve the spirit: and to resist the desires of the flesh. There there are divers offices: and many charitable services are performed. There everything has its time: and each one goes to his task out of obedience. There no man is allowed to idle:

but to each a measure of toil is assigned. There the weak are supported by the stronger: there the healthy visiting the sick rejoice to serve Christ. There when one fails, another takes his place: there the sound members take thought for the sickly. There the active toil for them that take leisure: there they, that take leisure in God, pray for them that toil. There while one reads, many are edified: there all respectively fulfilling their weekly offices, relieve one another, that they be not wearied. There a man has many to pray for him: and in his last hour to defend him against the devil. There he finds as many helpers as he has companions: to assist him in his need. There he falls happily asleep in the Lord; there he is speedily freed from Purgatory by the intercession of many. There after death he leaves as his heirs who will certainly be mindful of him at times; the servants of God whose devout pursuits shall be his joy in Heaven. There his toil and his edifying life shall not be forgotten: but shall profit as an example for many coming after. There those that follow are obliged to pray for them that go before: and to praise God for the good deeds of benefactors. There whatever good is performed: is considered as shared by all who rest therein. There those, who yet live, take thought for departed brethren that they may be loosed from their pains; and those, who are now reigning with Christ, supplicate for the wayfarers, that they may continue in good: and those, who still survive, long to join their brothers. There the good of the individual becomes the good of the community: there what is of time becomes eternal. There those that live together in time: shall rejoice together for eternity. A great therefore and a pleasant good: is the dwelling of many Devout in unity. Who perseveres in a holy Congregation unto the end, even if he be imperfect: because of the prayers of many, and the merits of the perfect by the mercy of God he shall attain a happy consummation. But who abandons a good Congregation: wandering as it were outside the harbour of perseverance and salvation, he exposes himself to the storms of the sea. For who separates himself from the midst of a Congregation: it is doubtful where he will yet persevere. The end will soon make clear: whether he departed moved by God, or by passion. Abide therefore in the midst of the holy Congregation: and the Lord will abide with thee. For He Himself saith: am in the midst of you: as he that serveth." And to His disciples He saith. are they who have continued with Me in My temptations." If thou art good: remain and edify others. If thou art a sinner and weak: remain to be edified by others. But whithersoever thou shalt go, know that the devil will be thy enemy: and thy passion will follow thee, even if thou shouldst be alone and enclosed. For often from light words and a fanciful raiment without: is known the condition of the mind, what vanity is nourished within.

AN EXAMPLE OF TWO BRETHREN

Two brethren once arrived at the house of a certain man, a noble and a prince of the land: for some matter concerning the interests of the monastery. The good prince therefore observing them closely: noted the exterior habit and behaviour of each. And when they were gone, this wise man said to his lady in private: without, however, openly detracting any one: "It seemed to me that one of those either has recently come there: or will soon want to depart." To whom the mistress in wonder said: "How do you know this?" He answered: "From the difference in garb and gesture, in words and behaviour: I guess the difference of life." A short time after therefore: the thing that was hidden was made manifest.

ANOTHER REMARKABLE EXAMPLE

A certain Devout being grievously tempted by the devil: went out from the Congregation of the Brothers to seek comfort in the world in idle games. Having forsaken therefore the lowly fellowship of the clerics: he frequently joined the company of laymen. One day, however, going out beyond the city gate, he commenced to play with his comrades for money; and playing for some time he lost his stake: and what is worse the repute of a good conscience. When at length the game of pyramid was ended: he was called upon to pay his debts without further delay. He refuses to pay the tricksters their gains: he resists violently, he endeavours to escape: he struggles and will yield nothing of his own accord. The players therefore, excited and crowding together round the dishonest debtor like rabid dogs against a wolf: shout, push, strike with the hands, curse with the words: "Give up, cheat, what thou owest." But when he would not yield to his persecutors: being exceedingly angry, they bestowed on him many hard blows for the few pence. When he had at length come to himself: he was brought back by some people into the town. He sent word therefore to the Devout Brethren, his fellow countrymen, beseeching them with many prayers to visit him stricken down by sickness: telling them the story of his miserable passion. For the music of worldly amusement had been changed: into the mourning of bitter affliction. When they had heard this, the gentle Brothers visit the sick man, compassionating the soul in affliction; nevertheless they severely reprimand him for the crime he has committed: telling him that he received blows well deserved, according to those gospel words of our Lord: "Go out quickly into the highways and hedges and compel them to come in." "For if," say they, "thou hadst remained in the Congregation: thou wouldst not have received so many wounds." Then he with much groaning: owned that he had done foolishly and sinned. “Therefore,” said he, “if I recover: by God’s help, I purpose to amend.” But many of the Brethren hearing of these misfortunes were seized with fear: and being rendered more constant made better progress, according to that of Solomon: “The wicked man being scourged: the fool shall be wiser.” It is good then to remain at home with the Brothers and to keep away from worldly company: and to undertake nothing without the superior’s advice: nor to extort permission to go out by false pretence or supplications. For that often causes regret in the end: which is ill obtained by our own whim. He who will make progress and persevere in the Congregation: ought to be open to his superior in confession: faithful in labour, true in word. Among the Brethren he should be modest, humble, silent, quiet: pious, well-behaved, patient, grateful, and obedient. These things make one dear to God: lovable to men and a trouble to no one.

ANOTHER OF A CERTAIN CLERIC OFTEN GOING ABROAD

A certain Cleric, who dwelt in a community of the Brothers for the sake of studies; often visited his friends in search of amusement: often also went to the places and houses of religious. The Brothers therefore and his fellow students: fearing danger for him from constant going abroad, said to him: “If thou wilt persevere in a good state, do not go out of the house so often: be on thy guard against visiting friends, and familiarity with women.” When therefore he had been often and gravely warned by many: and did not abandon his bad habit; at length the temptation grew stronger and he left the holy company: and returning to his friends, took to himself a wife and became wholly worldly and dissipated.

SERMON III

OF HUMBLY HEARING THE WORDS AND COUNSELS OF ELDERS

ASK thy father and he will declare to thee: thy elders and they will tell thee. Beloved brethren, listen willingly to the wholesome counsels of your elders; and be not wise in your own conceits: lest you fall into the snare of the devil and incur scandal to your soul. Search not things sublime; nor curiously examine the deeds of others: but what is the will of God, and what you have promised to observe: always keep in mind. A certain devout religious said: "He who holds his peace concerning the affairs of all others: has peace with all." O precious word: profitable to be ever kept in the soul. For the more a man is spread abroad without: the more is he lessened within. Let no man then, looking at others, neglect himself: having a care of himself before all, let him be silent as to the rest: which does not concern his charge. And so let every one, who wishes to be interior, say with the psalmist: "My soul is continually in my hands: and I have not forgotten Thy law." Whoever will make progress in the spirit: let him give himself often to prayer and the privacy of silence; let him shun many questions and the making of long discourses: but rather let him devoutly pray with holy David: "O Lord, to Thee have I fled: teach me to do Thy will." If you ask what is the will of God: blessed Paul plainly and clearly answers us all: "This is the will of God, your sanctification." What is this sanctification; if not to keep away from evil, and daily to exercise oneself in good? If you do not know what is more pleasing to God, and what you should do for greater profit; go at once and diligently ask of your superior, or of the more experienced elders: lest it befall you to abound in your own sense, and err. What is the cause that so many fall away from their first devotion; and make so little headway in true virtues? Because, alas! they depart little by little from the holy purpose of poverty and simplicity, which they received and learnt from the elders; and follow rather their own fancies, and devise new conveniences, dread things simple and lowly, seek the familiarity of men; desire to show their knowledge: and esteem themselves above even learned elders. And would that they would learn again the humble exercises of novices: and gratefully receive a little warning.

Brethren, let no man be ashamed to learn from the elders; let no man spurn to receive an edifying word from the juniors: for this is a praiseworthy sign of humility; this is a very good omen of spiritual progress: according to that proverb of Solomon: "A wise man shall hear and shall be wiser, and he that understandeth shall possess governments." Who wishes to be wise and to be accounted learned before he listens and learns: he shall long remain foolish in the midst of the wise. It is a true proverb: "Who will not hear the master like a good scholar: he shall be beaten with the obstinate like an unmannered ass."

Consider now in order from the writings of both Testaments, the holy fathers and doctors, the prophets and apostolic men resplendent in knowledge and virtues; how eager they were in life and in death to teach their children and subjects: how many secret things of God they foretold them concerning the future and heavenly goods under various figures and parables; thereby to render all their hearers well-disposed to observe the law: and to make them wishful to obtain all the divine promises both present and to come. For Moses, the chief teacher and lawgiver, spake thus: "Hear, O Israel, the commandments and judgements which I teach thee: that doing them thou mayest live. You shall not add to the word that I speak to you, neither shall you take away from it: and thou shalt teach them to thy children and children's children." And again in another place: "Thou shalt love the Lord thy God with thy whole heart and with thy whole soul: and with thy whole strength. And these words which I command thee this day shall be in thy heart, and thou shalt tell them to thy children: and thou shalt meditate upon them sitting in thy house, and walking on thy journey, sleeping and rising. And thou shalt bind them as a sign on thy hand; and they shall move between thy eyes: and thou shalt write them in the entry and on the doors of thy house." Behold what holy precepts and godly exercises of divine teaching are proposed to us by Moses: to be worthily followed also by all the faithful.

After holy Moses arose in his place Josue, a faithful minister chosen out of thousands: to whom the Lord said: "As I have been with Moses: so will I be with thee. Take courage and be very valiant; that thou mayest observe and do all the law, which Moses My servant commanded thee: and turn not from it to the right or to the left." And because Moses laid his hand upon him, he merited the divine blessing; and he was filled with the spirit of wisdom which is most necessary for good government in a state and multitude: and the children of Israel obeyed him as Moses according to the commandment of the Lord. Hearing this each Brother, novice or professed, ought to apply it as a profitable example to himself, humbly obeying his superior or senior Brother for God's sake, that he may deserve to have a heavenly blessing: because of his humility and ready obedience. For humble obedience merits a special grace from God; and it is protected from many snares of the devil: and it shall be excused in the judgement of the ill deeds and offences charged against it. Therefore I beseech you, younger ones, listen humbly to the seniors, who have long experience in many things; who have long borne in the Order the burden of the day and the heats; often wearied in body, often afflicted in mind. Whom God tried mightily in the fire of poverty as gold in the furnace of fire; and after long want and distress of heart He very often comforted them with the joy of the Holy Ghost and the sweetness of the Sacrament: as of old He fed the children of Israel in the desert with manna from Heaven.

It is read in the First Book of Kings, that Samuel, dear to God and men, when he was yet a small child, was offered by his holy mother Anna to God, and entrusted to the priest Heli to be instructed; that under his teaching he might be accustomed from boyhood humbly to serve God in the tabernacle of the altar: and in good conduct according to the law of God gradually be made perfect to receive higher and more holy things. Which also was done with the gracious favour of God. And he in everything to be done and decided strove to obey at once the priest, as the vicar of God: so that he did not presume even to go to sleep without his leave. For called thrice by the Lord in the night: he at once arose from his bed. And because as yet he did not know the divine revelation, readily he ran to the presence of the priest which was known to him: and submitted to the judgement of his superior the voice, which he heard; trusting more to the experience of the old man and the advice of the priest: than to his own innocence which might easily be deceived in the secret things of God or foolishly lifted up. O what will this child be in the future: who was so repectful and obedient to his elder in the opening of life. Certainly as he grew in age he increased also in the grace of a more sublime revelation: so that after the death of his priest he became the judge of the whole people; and anointed kings by the order of the Lord: and by the power of his prayer vanquished the force of the enemy. For all knew from Dan to Bersabee: that Samuel was a faithful prophet of the Lord. Who often calling the people together, and reminding them of the very numerous blessings of God, rebuked them for the foolish worship of idols: and for their great ingratitude after so many favours bestowed. And because they had often offended God: therefore they deserved to be most grievously chastised by their foes. Then he earnestly calls back to the observance of the holy law all them that err, and says: "Put away the strange gods from among you; and prepare your hearts unto the Lord, and serve Him only: and He will deliver you out of the hands of your enemies."

David also, the king, powerful and holy, anointed by Samuel with holy oil prince of the people: when he had mightily ruled for many years the nation of Israel; before his death called Solomon his son to him: and charged him saying: "I am going the way of all flesh. Take thou courage and show thyself a man, and keep the charge of the Lord thy God: to walk in His ways, and observe His ceremonies, and His precepts, and judgements, and testimonies: as it is written in the law of Moses." Again in a certain psalm inspired by the Holy Ghost, instructing the people commended to him, and urging them to the worship of God he prays and saith: "Attend, O my people, to my law: incline your ear to the words of my mouth. How great things He commanded to our fathers that they should make the same known to their children: that another generation might know them. The children that should be born and should rise up: and should declare them to their children. That they may put their hope in God, and may not forget the works of the Lord: and may seek His commandments." Behold how devout an admonition of the glorious king; to the keeping of the holy law.

Solomon also the most wise of kings following his father's footsteps: among many proverbial sayings instructing youth speaks thus: "Hear, ye children, the instruction of a father: and attend that you may know prudence. I will give you a good gift: forsake not my law. For I also was my father's son, tender and as an only son in the sight of my mother: and he taught me and said: 'Let thy heart receive my words: keep my commandments and thou shalt live. Get wisdom, get prudence: forsake her not and she shall keep thee.' " Behold how profitable a lesson the Wise Man delivers to youth and especially to you novices, who have entered the school of God: that by the help of God you may progress in virtues even to old age.

It is also read in the first Book of the Maccha-bees, of Mathathias, a most noble man and a most unyielding defender of the law; that on fire with the zeal of God and powerfully aided by the help of God and men, he drove the wicked and the forsakers of the law of the ancients from his bounds: and according to his strength brought back befittingly the neglected statutes of the early fathers to a holy observance pleasing to God. Who in all his warlike deeds aimed at no other end; but that the honour and worship of God should be most firmly established in the holy laws: and that the desolate people by serving God should enjoy a happy peace; and with sincere hearts should worship God almighty with unbounded exultation: and with joyous voices should praise Him together. He at length, after many glorious deeds of good works, being at the point of death, and anxious with a father's love for the future, lest the good commenced with devout endeavour should perish through sloth; having called to his side his sons and friends who had zeal for God, he strengthens their hearts in most excellent words with many examples of holy men gone before: and earnestly urging and begging them all to perseverance in the good way on which they had entered, he said: "Now, therefore, O my sons, be ye zealous for the law: and give your lives for the covenant of your fathers. And call to remembrance the works of the fathers, which they have done in their generations: and you shall receive great glory and an everlasting name."

Our Saviour also the Lord Jesus Christ, having accomplished the mystery of our redemption by His Passion and cross, after His blessed resurrection appearing frequently to His disciples, among many sacred discourses, whereby He wisely and minutely instructed them: He uttered these parting and wholesome words. "Go ye," He said, "into the whole world and preach the gospel to every creature: and teach all nations to observe all things whatsoever I have commanded you." O happy and meritorious obedience: which regards nothing else than the eager fulfilment of the good pleasure and will of the heavenly Father. O how holy the soul, which strives to resign itself: and to conform its whole life to the actions of Christ. Truly a most excellent pattern of a good life: Jesus Christ left to us all. He is the master of all: He the book and rule of religious; He the commentary of monks: He the text and glossary of decrees. He is the pattern of life for clerics, the instruction of laymen; the light of the faithful, the joy of the just, the glory of the angels: the end and consummation of all the desires of the saints.

It is also read in the Acts of the Apostles, of most blessed Paul the apostle: that in the beginning of his conversion a heavenly voice said to him: "Arise, and go into the city: and there it shall be told thee what thou must do." Who immediately arose and obeyed the voice of God; and became a holy and great preacher throughout the world: who before had been a persecutor of the churches. He has shown a pattern of perfect renunciation to all religious: but he has especially left an example of obedience to the newly converted: that they say every hour with Paul, "Lord, what will thou have me to do?" And as then all who had known him were astounded at his sudden conversion: so also now all the wise of the world, wherever Christ be named, wonder and rejoice at his doctrine. Therefore on fire with divine love: he urged all to the love of Christ, saying: "Be followers of me, dearly beloved, as I also am of Christ." Of whom it is written in the Acts of the Apostles: that he was sent with Barnabas to preach the word of God to the gentiles: and converted many to the faith of

Christ. And after some days Paul said again to Barnabas: "Let us return and visit the brethren in all the cities wherein we have preached the word of the Lord, to see how they do: whether they are progressing or failing in their good beginnings." And again: "But Paul choosing Silas as a suitable companion for the work of preaching, went through Syria and Cilicia, confirming the churches: commanding them to keep the precepts of the apostles and the ancients."

Lo, brethren, you have now heard many good things, how solicitous the saints were in their day, to teach their children and subjects, to walk in the holy precepts of God: what examples also of holy conduct they left to their successors: which they themselves had first heard and learnt from the fathers and the ancients. So do you also, dearly beloved, as shoots of olive planted in the house of the Lord, stand in obedience and the discipline of the cloister; hold to the traditions of the elders and the statutes of the General Chapter: drawn up by the Definitors under divine inspiration for your salvation. Receive gratefully the warnings of your superiors: and patiently bear their reproofs: for it is better that they should correct you now: than that the devil hereafter should more grievously punish and mock you. For if now for Christ's sake you humbly yield to the advice of the elders, and forsake your own opinion; then you shall have great peace: and by the grace of Christ you shall receive eternal blessedness. Amen.

SERMON IV

OF HOLDING GOOD DISCOURSES TOGETHER

HERE there are two or three gathered together in My name: there am I in the midst of them, saith the Lord. Give heed, beloved brethren, to the presence of Christ in every place wheresoever you gather together, whether to pray or to labour; neither let one hinder another: or offend by a word or sign of levity. If there, leave given, it be permitted you at times to speak; let your discourse be of God and of devout matters from the holy scriptures: which may edify you in virtue, and comfort you in troubles. Thus did the holy fathers of old in Egypt: when they had come together for counsel and remedies unto the overcoming of temptations. But shun talking about the news of the world and the various conditions of men; nor rashly judge any secular: for God will judge all them that work iniquity. Let it be no interest to you then to think of temporal things, nor to converse about them: but only of spiritual progress in virtues, and the cures for your vices. Leave all exterior things and the business of the house to be ruled by God and arranged by your superiors: who will render an account in the judgement of the things committed to them. Be you contented and grateful for the service daily rendered you, satisfied with your wage in moderate food and clothing: seeking not fanciful things, nor superfluous, nor new, nor soft: but, as good simple sons of God living amid the brethren without complaint and dispute: out of humility think yourselves unworthy of all these blessings. Let your mind be fervent in desires of the heavenly kingdom: and in devout exercises let one strive to outstrip another; and take pleasure in knowing and thinking of nothing but Christ and Him crucified: so that for love and compassion of the Crucified all things of the world and the flesh may be turned into disgust; and the toil of penance seem short and easy to you: and the discipline of the regular life be changed into sweetness and the joy of a good conscience every day. For then Christ shall be in the midst of you praying and discoursing together; teaching you to despise earthly things and to love the heavenly: and manfully struggle against the temptations of the devil, and curb the passions of the flesh. For wherefore have you come from the world; if not that your whole hope should be in God, and your heart above in heaven? Since therefore you have chosen to renounce the world, and to serve Christ in the cloister: flee worldly men, forsake the friends of the flesh; for they may hinder you in your devotion, and by their speech draw you to hurtful desires: and bring no profit to your soul. The more seldom and the more briefly you speak to men: the safer is it for the guard of your heart and mouth. It is greatly to your honour and the good name of the Order, if out of respect for guests you appear modest and silent in their presence: for you will edify more by your good conduct: than by the polish of your speech. From one unguarded word they impute to you frivolity and indiscretion: and under the religious habit they conclude that a fox is hiding, and pretending to be a sheep.

Let your words therefore be few, profitable and prudent: for an idle word will not pass unpunished with God. To guard against this, silence is to be loved and kept: and therefore was it wholesomely instituted in religion by the holy fathers of old, and by our recent superiors. In fine, in no state or Order will peace and discipline abide: if there be no strictness of silence, the friend of quiet: which is the food of devotion, the closing of contention, the flight of vanity. In silence you may learn: how and to whom you should speak. By idle words the soul becomes dissipated and instable: scarcely able to return to its interior after long mourning and tears. But from godly discourses spring love of God, edification of the neighbour: hatred of the world, desire for the kingdom of Heaven: sorrow for sin, the heat of charity, the bridling of cupidity: and the renewal of the whole inward man in the mirror of the most holy life of our Saviour. For He deigns to be present to those that speak of Him: He is nigh unto all that call upon Him. By holy discourse He arouses the slothful, strengthens the feeble; aids them that fight manfully, crowns the conquerors: terrifies by punishments, exhorts by good examples: comforts by the promise of gifts, rejoices by grace freely bestowed in time: beatifies by the manifestation of the eternal glory of Heaven, as witnesses the psalmist: "I shall be satisfied," he says, "when Thy glory shall appear." So loving and merciful is Jesus: so sweet and mild is Christ; that if any man prepare a place for Him in his heart, without doubt he will freely show him the light of His grace: and will sup with him. If one is alone and reads or prays: Jesus desires to make a second. If two together read or chant: Jesus wishes to be a third. Nor will be the supplication of these gathered in the name of Jesus, who in good faith humbly and devoutly pray, be void; if, however, in everything which they beseech or desire, they seek

His good pleasure, and renounce their own will: saying that most acceptable word of Christ: "Father, not my will: but Thine be ever done. Amen."

SERMON V

OF HAVING PATIENCE AMID THE SLOTHFUL AND PERVERSE

SAY to the faint-hearted: "Take courage, and fear not." Beloved brethren, be not disturbed if at times some failings, which pain you, are found in religious: or it some depart from the congregation of the good: or if they live with them lukewarmly because of the temptations of the devil: which they suffer daily in the service of God. For these sad assaults of human weakness also befell before our days; as we read of many holy and religious men: who are now honoured by many throughout the world. We are indeed frail, and prone to evil, therefore is it needful that our evil ways be straitened by statutes: and that like wild colts we be fastened to the stake of the holy cross for the Name of Jesus; lest, living according to our own desire, we turn aside from the righteous path of the saints: who entered the kingdom of Heaven by the narrow gate. Let us therefore mutually pray that God may aid and strengthen us in our every trial and temptation: and guard us from the assault and deceit of the enemy, who goes around everywhere seeking whom he may devour; and by what device he may draw a man from the midst of the congregation into the world: and from the world to hell. There there is no redemption, but everlasting horror dwelleth: there the souls seek death and find it not: there they are tormented day and night in fire and brimstone: because here they refused to do a little penance: and spent their time so foolishly and fruitlessly.

Brethren, let us not seek the rest and ease of the flesh like men of the world; but toil and pain for our sins: let us resist vice by often fasting, praying, reading, meditating. Assuredly, we shall not have peace and quiet upon earth, wherever we may be, or wherever also we may go to seek comfort: or to ease our weariness, or to lessen the burden of our labour: unless we turn ourselves to Christ by prayer and sorrow for sins, with a firm purpose of always doing penance: so that by this light toil and short pain we may be able to escape the torment of everlasting fire. Our peace and the repose of a good life consist in much patience, according to the life of Christ and the examples of the saints; not in a long flight by waterless ways: nor in a vessel passing over the seas. Jonas the Prophet wished to flee from the face of the Lord: he went up into a ship, but it profited him nothing. He gave himself to sleep, he sought repose: but he did not find it. He thought that he was concealed, but God made manifest the hidden one: stirred up a storm, and moved the ocean. Then the sailors rouse up the sleeper, rebuke him and cast him into the water: who, immediately swallowed by a fish as a runaway and as disobedient, is imprisoned in the belly of a whale for his fault. Shut up therefore in this close prison, he cried and prayed to the Lord to be delivered from such great perils of the sea and from the confinement of the fish. At length, however, destitute of all human succour, he recognized in his affliction that it is impossible to escape the hand of God: and that to obey the divine commands is the most assured salvation of the soul. Let us therefore not flee from the toils and hardships that arise in religion for our salvation, of which we knew not before: but let us stand firm, strive manfully, obey readily: pray frequently, toil diligently, keep silence willingly. Let us bear with ourselves patiently for Christ's sake, as all the saints have done: who, having endured things more grievous, now rejoice in Heaven and say; "We have passed through fire and water: and Thou hast brought us out into an eternal refreshment." We live amid many perils: and they, that tempt and trouble us, sleep not nor rest: but seek to ensnare us and to hinder us from the good we have commenced. Let us however not lose heart, nor cease to pray and to cry to Christ: even if we are often lukewarm and dry, and for distress of soul know not what we ought to do: for maybe God proves us in a few things: whether we really love Him not only in words but also in deeds and blows. Therefore when rough winds arise, let us not yield, but set our hands to the oars: let us seize our spiritual weapons, let us lift up our saddened soul, begin anew: and strive to struggle, much more strongly than we have done, against the flesh, against the world and against the devil. For the harder the fight: the more glorious the crown: and the more frequent the annoyance of the sufferer: the more praiseworthy the virtue of him that is patient. A great hindrance is cowardice of heart, to lose confidence speedily in adversity: to neglect one's holy purpose, to think of the life in the world: to dwell in fancy upon the presence of friends, to think of the agreeableness of comrades; all which things are emptiness and folly: as the swift end of all pleasure and honour shows. Our life, brethren, and religion undertaken for God consist in daily combat: namely, to struggle against bad habits, which everywhere and always, in the choir, in the dormitory, in silence, in labour pursue and tempt us: would that they never overcame us. Therefore it is not wonderful, if sometimes we slip and are wounded: if lightly we offend and are offended, in words, in deeds of our own and of others. We are men, not angels; mortals we are and frail sinners: exiles we are and pilgrims, not citizens of Heaven; inconstant and prone to vice: not yet perfect in grace, or blessed in glory. This thought ought to humble us, not lift up to pride of mind; but by our own weakness to lead us to trust in the divine mercy and loving-kindness: without which we are unable to commence or accomplish anything, witness our Lord, Who saith: "For without Me you can do nothing." For our own weakness very greatly weighs us down: but the divine inspiration and heavenly visitation again raise up them that faint and strengthen unto well-doing: and He lovingly disposes for the profit of our salvation that we may be able to bear whatever unexpected things befall us: and with a just and secret judgement dispenses all things. For He has care of us all: from the beginning of life unto the end of death. For He who made us will not abandon us, if we do not forsake Him: but will make with temptation issue that we may be able to resist and bear its onslaught. Let us say therefore to Him with the holy man in the psalm: when we are attacked by the wicked enemy: "Be Thou my helper, Lord God: forsake me not." And again with all confidence of mind let us cry to Christ in Heaven: "My eyes are ever towards the Lord: for He shall pluck my feet out of the snare." But peace and perfect repose are in Heaven, not on earth: for here all things are in movement and fear and frequent distress. Therefore strong patience is supremely necessary for us in this fragile life: which is naught else but a daily struggle against vice. For whether a man be in his own house or in another, whether among acquaintance or familiar friends: something will speedily befall him which will displease him and disturb the tranquillity of the soul, secure nowhere. Let each then set himself to patience as best he can: and patiently bear whatever God shall permit: and thus he shall have more ample peace. If he be injured and blamed by anyone: let him overcome his pride, and learn to suffer reproach: and he shall find great favour with God and never-ending glory. Let him grieve that he has sinned and not borne contempt of himself with sufficient patience: and let him humbly crave pardon for all his offences: and God will freely forgive him all.

Beloved brethren, lose not courage, nor add evils to evils: but at once when your conscience accuses you, hasten to the remedy of confession. God is the only one: Whom sin befalls not. For in His angels He found wickedness: and a great portion of them fell from Heaven by pride: because they gave not glory to God for the gifts bestowed upon them. The first man in Paradise was tempted and deceived: and because of the sin of disobedience he was cast out of the place of pleasure into the wretchedness of this world. What wonder then if some weak brother, grievously tempted by the devil and the flesh, or rebuked by many for his failing sometimes errs, and sins, or becomes impatient: when man well established in Paradise fell, where he had so many helps and no hindrances? Many holy and just men in the Old Law were often tempted and persecuted by evil men: but they patiently bore with the wicked: and became better by means of their adversities. At times, however, by the will of God they resisted the wicked; and wrought a just vengeance upon the impious: lest the good weighed down in tribulation should be too much dejected. For some fell overcome by a sudden temptation: others stricken by a long illness, were humbled in their evil deeds: and those whom wealth and honours had uplifted: sorrow and shame brought back to a knowledge of their own weakness. Many also after a grievous fall repenting quickly arose the stronger: and laudibly finished their life in holy ways.

In the days of Christ and His apostles the good were mingled with the bad, in the city, on the road: in the house, in the wilderness. Some believed in Christ and praised His works: others contradicted Him, and complained of Him. Some also, misunderstanding His mystic words, laughed Him to scorn: and because He righteously reproved their vices: they enviously calumniated His true and holy miracles. Even while Christ was discoursing and present there befell among the disciples some anger and quarrel as to which of them should be the greater and first in prelacy and in ruling of the nascent Church: which He gathered together from divers places and peoples and especially from the poor and simple: whom the loving and lowly Master by word and example recalled to the concord of peace by the way of humility with a gentle reproof, saying: "Unless you be converted and become as little children: you shall not enter into the kingdom of Heaven." And again: "And he that will be first among you: shall be the servant of you all." Behold, dearly beloved, by these examples of humility and patience, what are the bases of all virtues; a simple and obedient brother can arrive at the kingdom of Heaven with a secure conscience without many arguments and subtle words: and escape the eternal torments of hell, by patiently bearing all wrongs whatever, unjustly wrought him by the perverse. It is seen, then, from the foregoing that in all places and times of the saints there were good and evil, believers and unbelievers; devout and dissolute, benevolent and perverse, spiritual and carnal; and the good by their patience made daily progress unto better: and the evil vanished like smoke in their wickedness and desires. But God, the Creator of all and the searcher of the ages, from the beginning even to the end, has known how to dispose the causes of each in such manner; that for the good all things work together unto good: and for the wicked all things end in eternal punishment. From which evils now and for ever may the loving and merciful Lord save us, the just judge and patient rewarder: Who is above all God blessed for ever. Amen.

SERMON VI

OF THE NIGHT WATCHES AGAINST THE ASSAULT OF SLEEPINESS

SIMON, sleepest thou? Could you not watch one hour with Me? Watch ye, and pray: that you enter not into temptation. This voice, beloved brethren, is the voice of the heavenly King and our Saviour Jesus Christ: Who urges His soldiers to watch in the camp against the temptations of the devil, the enemy of the human race. What therefore the Lord watchfully addresses to blessed Peter and the other disciples: this also undoubtedly He says to us all. Therefore, when the sacristan comes round at midnight and arouses us: let us be wakeful at once at the sound of the bell: and make ourselves ready by devout prayers to enter the choir: and hasten to meet the heavenly Bridegroom with burning torches. Let us endeavour, dearly beloved, manfully to cast off the sloth of the body: and sleepiness from our eyes. Let us lift up our hands to Heaven, to praise our Creator with joyous voices and pure minds: lest perchance the most cunning enemy prevail against us: and mock at some gaping, others singing but little, others out of tune in their voices. It is a very bad habit of some and it is to be hoped not of many, which I should be ashamed to say; who in the dormitory or in bed lie long awake idly dreaming: and in the church and in choir slumber for lack of devotion. These often harm themselves and others: they neither serve Christ manfully: nor pray faithfully for benefactors and the afflicted. For they offend God seriously, rising slothfully, often coming late: chanting lukewarmly, mispronouncing the words, often yawning, carelessly looking about them: paying little attention, making the inclinations heedlessly, wearying of the length of the psalms, and hastening to the finish. They rejoice at the signal for the refectory, they dread the bell for chapter: they hasten to a gossip, they enter their cell but slowly: they have little interest in their work, they are eager over dishes well prepared. All these are signs of little devotion, of great ingratitude: and of deep shame. Alas, the fear of God is not before their eyes: nor the love of God in their heart, nor His praise in their mouth: but perfidy in their voice, and luke-warmness in their deed. Where is God, where the angels: where all the saints of God? Where is the superior, where the sacristan, where the cantor; where the lector, where the suscitator? Everything fades away before the eyes of the sleeper. "Awake, ye just, and sin not," says the apostle. ye and pray," saith the Lord: "lest Satan tempt you, idle through want of spirit." For he goeth about day and night seeking whom he may devour: how to deceive the simple, distract the devout: and disturb the peaceful. He is very glad if anyone does not chant, or reads ill: if he closes his eyes and slumbers: if with unguarded eyes he looks about and neglects himself He is speedily at hand to snatch the verse from the mouth of the sleepy: and to throw into his sack the fragments of words. O silly brother of the race of sleepers and of the number of the foolish virgins, whose lamps, we read, went out in the night: if thou dost not fear God, or respect the angels, or feel shame to scandalize thy brethren; why dost thou not dread the devil laying snares for thee, who diligently records in his book all the neglected and imperfect words? For as the holy angels present devout prayers to God, and love and praise them that sing fervently; so Satan with his followers lies in wait for them that pray, to distract and hinder those who sing psalms together in unison: and to have points not a few against them, of which to accuse and punish them. But since thou dost not heed or fear so cruel a thief, so crafty a spy, so severe a creditor, so unsparing an accuser, and harsh executioner, and seldom or but little dost weigh the evils to come and the pains of hell: therefore thou growest weary and dost slumber: and as one dead in the grave dost lie still and silent. There is no toil so heavy, no sorrow so bitter: but that it becomes lighter by comparison with the fire of hell. Alas, what shalt thou do at the moment of death: when the devil runs to meet thee with a terrible countenance and breathing fury? Where then the faithful friends: where the fine banquets and all the honours of the world? Wilt thou escape these terrors: and not fear the demons? Arise, watch, pray: sing, read, toil. Be silent before wrongs, bear injuries, love insults: spurn honours, forgive sinners. Let not the mourning of the damned depart from thy eyes, the fearful clamour of the demons: the most grievous banishment from the presence of God and the joyous fellowship of the saints. Thou art often afraid seeing the fire of a burning furnace: thou tremblest at thunder and lightning: thou dreadest storms, and great frosts: and dost scarcely dare to go to sleep and abide in thy cell. Since thou hast heard and read that many have come to an end by a sudden accident and sickness: why dost thou not fear that the like may happen thee? Know that more terrible torments threaten after death. Set in thy mind the things that are naturally dreadful, namely a blazing vessel full of pitch, stinking of sulphur: think of roaring lions, dogs biting, serpents hissing: toads gnawing, dragons devouring: and thou shalt more speedily overcome the vile sins brought thee by the devil to stain thy heart: and thou shalt drive farther from thee sloth of mind, sleepiness of body, and the desire of most empty praise. I tell thee that long vigils, long lessons, the daily Hours, silence, toil, and fast make a short Purgatory: and bring great joy, after the space of three or four hours. It is strange that thou dost so easily feel weariness in the choir chanting or reading: and dost not grow weary with long conversing, or hearing news of the world. Understand that this is the work of the devil: who strives in every way to hinder the divine worship: and to draw thee away from the church and the gathering of them that sing psalms: that he may have a companion to burn for ever in hell. Then they shall yell and howl for exceeding heat and pain: who do not now praise God in heart and mouth with great fervour. If it pleases thee to discourse with a friend for the sake of receiving some relief: how much more oughtest thou to hasten and pant to hear the things of God: to speak with God in hymns and canticles, leaving aside all other cares and fancies. But since facts often move more than words: some examples are to be added at the end of the sermon, for the sake of instruction. Imitate the good which pleases: be on thy guard against the evil which displeases.

AN EXAMPLE

A certain brother began to sleep a little at Matins. Noticing which, the brother seated next to him: quietly cast into his ear just this word: "Hell!" On hearing this, suddenly terrified and awakened: he cast off all drowsiness from him. Think therefore, slothful one, of hell: and thou wilt not slumber in choir, tired through weariness.

ANOTHER

Another brother also was singing but little, and when his neighbour did not hear his voice: he remonstrated with him that just then Matins were being sung. "Simon, sleepest thou?" And he, aroused by these words, became aware that he was remarked in his drowsiness: and in surprise and shame he was abashed before him that rebuked him.

ANOTHER

There was a certain brother in the Order of Regulars devout to God and well read: an artistic singer, and a zealous lover of the divine praise. He was speaking once familiarly with another brother on the sweetness of the divine chant: and of the solemn office which is performed in the church on the chief festivals. He said therefore to him by way of edification to encourage his weakness: that he might cheerfully sing in choir. "Brother, praise be to God, I have never had weariness in the Divine Office: however long it might be. For on the Feast of Palms, although compared with other days the divine service seems very long: nevertheless I was not weary of the length of the singing: but I felt myself so ready to sing, that if anyone had wished to begin the whole from the beginning again: I should willingly have commenced and chanted with him." Hearing this, the aforesaid brother was edified: and rendered more eager for the chant. This elder should be well believed; for he was always among the first to come to choir, he seldom went out, if he went out for some need he speedily returned: while there he faithfully helped according to his power, and he did not turn his eyes to other matters.

ANOTHER

Another brother of the same Order, on fire with the zeal of God, struggled hard against drowsiness: and did violence to himself as follows. For weighed down by sleep in choir, he pulled out the hairs of his head with his hand: he roughly rubbed his beard, he pricked his nose with a pen, he made his eyes smart with spittle: and sometimes he placed under his chin a hard piece of wood, that he might drive away sleep. And when he felt the motions of the flesh, he thought on the flames of the fire of hell: and he sharply tore the skin of his body with his finger nails, and inflicted red wounds on his prurient flesh: until the illicit movement, aroused by the devil, wholly ceased.

SERMON VII

OF GUARDING THE MOUTH AND DILIGENCE IN LABOUR WITH OBEDIENCE TO THE SUPERIOR

A GOOD man out of a good treasure bringeth forth good things. Beloved brethren, you should always have something good concerning God and holy Writ stored up in your heart; and in your external labour repeat the sweet words of Christ: to strengthen you in the burden of your toil. Turn over earnestly the devout psalms and hymns in the silence of your mouth: lest the devil discover you wandering within and idle, unprofitably occupied about the doings of others: for a heart unstable and empty of good thoughts, is the devil's nest. Weigh your words before you speak: lest you utter something foolish which may offend your hearers, and you may grieve to have said: because you have not observed the bounds of discretion. If you do not know how to speak wisely; strive nevertheless to hold your peace with humility and modesty: according to that of Solomon: "A fool, if he will hold his peace: shall be accounted wise."

Time is given to work well, not to idle: nor to gossip; nor to jest. Suffer not then any time to pass away without the fruit of good work: for if you have permission to speak: you have not however to utter anything useless. For as you are to render an account before God in the judgement of every idle word: so also of every time and moment ill or carelessly spent. But according to the different seasons and feasts by day and night exercises suited to the time should be taken up: and good purposes should be more fervently enkindled. Nevertheless for the good of obedience and the service of brotherly charity, all private matters should be neglected: nor is any singular practice of devotion to be preferred to holy obedience and the common profit. For thus Christ left the Temple and the doctors of the Law; and obeyed His Mother and Joseph like a good son subject to his parents: as an example for all religious. He who exercises himself well in this, and daily strives and labours to overcome himself: he will be most gloriously crowned because he hath striven lawfully. For all good works performed out of simple obedience for God's sake, are most pleasing to God: and worthy of a very great reward to be for ever crowned in Heaven. For the renunciation of our own will with true humility of heart subject to the prelate and the advice of the superior: surpasses all temporal gain and arguments of utility, and is resplendent with everlasting praise. For as nothing is more precious than a good will, nor more at rest than free submission: so nothing is more vile than self will with the swelling of pride. Hence Solomon saith in praise of obedience. "An obedient man shall speak of victory." It is a great struggle to overcome oneself: a noble triumph to bow the neck of pride; to leave one's own opinion, to lay aside one's own wisdom: and in nothing to wish to show oneself. Every man who freely obeys for God's sake, does the work of a mighty warrior; because he fights against himself: and slays the motions of his own will with the sword of the fear of God. And so he shall receive a crown of everlasting glory with the martyrs: because he has manfully struggled and conquered. Whoever therefore humbly obeys a superior, or even an inferior, and willingly submits his opinion to the opinion of another: he loses nothing, but yielding to the other, gains the more. Every man who thus overcomes and humbles himself: treads upon the head of proud Lucifer, who suggests things contrary to humility: that a man give not way to another, but turn himself to cunning arguments. Why this? Lest keeping silence, he be lowered outwardly, and seem as a fool or an ignoramus: because he knows not how to defend himself, or suffers himself to be vanquished. Alas pride, how blind and foolish always: how far thou wanderest from the kingdom of God: and rushest headlong to the gates of hell. O what good and praiseworthy things have been said of thee, holy humility, always ready to obey; for to thee are opened the portals of Heaven: to see the glorious countenance of Jesus Christ. Let it not then be burdensome to anyone, nor seem unworthy to obey man for God's sake in things lawful and righteous: while Christ has been made obedient even to the shame of the cross. Truly, brethren, if a man will obey and serve a brother for God's flake, he shows God the greatest honour in his submission: and in the end he shall have Christ as the recompense of his labour and the rewarder of his holy subjection speaking thus: "What you did to one of these My least brethren: you did to me." For without obedience and brotherly love: our works are either little, or nothing. But with humble obedience: even worthless and small services rendered a brother please God. A truly and perfectly obedient man does not tarry when called: he does not excuse himself when busy or wearied: for he fears to incur the displeasure of God: if he follow not the voice of him that commands according to his power. Whether therefore the obedient man toils or prays, whether he reads or writes: whether he is silent or speaks, whether he watches or rests, whether he eats, or fasts: all things are accounted to him unto good from the merit of holy obedience. For in performing or in leaving all his acts he merits equally well, if he fully resign himself within: if herein he truly seek and aim at the good pleasure and honour of God. And he progresses the more fully and is the more acceptably pleasing to God; the more quickly and readily he fulfills: that which the will of the superior declares should be done. And if he knew better and the precept were more clearly made manifest to him: without any wavering, he should show himself most prompt to obey God and His vicar. Therefore the truly obedient man is always joyful, and has great trust in God; Whose will He desires to accomplish at all times: from Whom he doubts not he will receive a never-ending reward with the elect, singing in heart and mouth: "My heart is ready, O God: my heart is ready." And again. "I am ready and am not troubled: that I may keep Thy commandments."

SERMON VIII

OF SHUNNING VAINGLORY, AND THAT PRAISE IS TO BE RENDERED TO GOD ALONE

SO let your light shine before men that they may see your good works: and glorify your Father Who is in Heaven. Beloved brethren, when you do any good, be not lifted up, do not vainly boast; but humble your heart before God: lest on account of vainglory and self complacency you lose heavenly glory and the reward eternal. Every good action is to be attributed to God: not to your industry or power. Strive to wish to please God alone: and to give good example to the neighbour, in the observance of the regular discipline; lest the devil find whereby to grievously accuse you: and urge that you are like to sepulchres whitened without. Of what profit the vain praise of men; when within an evil conscience accuses of sins? The proud man and ambitious of temporal glory has toil without fruit: and unless he speedily repent and deeply humble himself: he will heap up a sum of greater punishment. Outside the charity of God and the neighbour the works praised by men are of no avail; but they are as empty vessels having no oil: and as lamps giving no light in the dark. Certainly they are the foolish virgins: who for any good work or word seek the praises of men. But they are the wise, who stand in fear, and guard in true humility the little good which they do: all likewise that they know and understand, and bring to effect, or purpose to make better: this they attribute with truth to God, the giver of all good things. Otherwise they are thieves and robbers: thieves because they unlawfully usurp the glory and honour of God; robbers because by vainly boasting they wound their own soul: and by taking pride they destroy the grace of God.

Who is just and prudent? He who has God ever before his eyes; who always thinks on good things: always speaks good things: always does good things, while he lives and is able. Do not, brethren, take pride from this that you know and read much: or because you have been long in the way of God and in religion. You should rather grieve that you have made so little progress in virtues: and would that you had still the first-fruits of the sweetness of a beginner, and so felt. However, you must not lose heart, or cease from your good endeavours: but with all humility beseech the divine assistance: that God deign to inspire you with fresh fervour. For as long as a man dwells in the present condition, he is instable, and liable to fall from good to evil: and on the other hand he is capable of being brought back from evil to good. Whence the wise king Solomon saith: "There is no just man upon earth: that doth good, and sinneth not." And blessed John, the most beloved disciple of Jesus, says in his epistle: that no man may vainly glory in his justice and purity. "If we say that we have no sin, we deceive ourselves: and the truth is not in us." Let no man therefore excuse himself as if he were blameless, and clear of fault: for in many things we all offend, saith blessed James the Apostle. For either knowingly a man sins, or unknowingly: either willingly or unwillingly, either from weakness, or from a perverse will: either from fear or from love, either from despair or presumption: either from frivolity of mind, or from habit, or from lukewarmness; either drawn by company, or puffed up by singularity: either stirred by anger, or carried away by concupiscence. By these passions and various desires, as by contrary winds, the heart of man is often moved and disturbed: and because of these storms of the world, very seldom does a man attain the harbour of repose. For there is scarcely a day or a night, an hour or an interval so brief and good: but in something a man errs or grows lukewarm, or commits negligences. For all which it behoves to pray without ceasing; that the loving God may mercifully forgive us all our evils: of which we have been guilty in word or deed or thought. And because no man is free from stain; therefore with humility and sorrow of heart speedy recourse must be had to the remedy of confession: and with greater watchfulness care be taken for the future against every occasion of evil thoughts. It behoves a man to strive to guard against evil in the beginning, lest the wily serpent find a small opening: and at length violently thrust in his whole head and tail. The heart of man cannot rest; but it is occupied either in good or in evil: as frequent experience teaches. And as much as a man loves good and pursues virtue: so much he hates evil and detests vice: because contraries cannot dwell together in one home. But no man shall find repose of heart whatever he may have or desire; unless he seek and hold in enjoyment God the true and supreme good: and use temporal things with moderation unto meriting the eternal kingdom of God.

Therefore, brethren, seek Christ in humility now: that hereafter you may see Him in His majesty. Seek now His grace by prayers with unfeigned tears: that cleansed from all stains, you may be worthy to see His face in Heaven.

Seek now Christ in the law and the prophets concealed under figures: that hereafter you may know all the secrets of the scriptures perfectly without books and masters: as it is said by the apostle Paul: "We see now through a glass in a dark manner: but then face to face."

But to possess the supreme good with the elect of God, who can be meet and worthy? Assuredly the truly humble, the perfectly obedient, mild and patient: grieving much for sins, strongly resisting vice: spurning the glory of the world, accounting himself nothing; seldom in things exterior, assiduous in interior: cold towards the things of earth, on fire for the things of Heaven: gentle to bear with others, vigorous in chastising self: easy to forgive, difficult to provoke: anxious every hour to watch over his heart: slow to go outside, joyful of soul to abide at home. Blessed he who turns over these things in his mind: and most speedily returns to his interior. Blessed he who suffers nothing temporal, nothing carnal, nothing impure, nothing swollen to enter the sanctury of his heart: nor permits the like to tarry there. Blessed he who knows many good things and does what he says; for now he has great peace: and hereafter with Christ he shall equally obtain a more blessed glory. Which may He deign to bestow upon us with all His saints: Who is above all God, blessed for ever. Amen.

SERMON IX

OF THE RISK OF MANY EVILS FROM MUCH BANDYING OF WORDS

DO not multiply to speak lofty things boasting. Beloved brethren, hold this verse firmly in your mind, and beware of speaking of sublime matters; lest the devil tempt you to vainglory: and you lose your time given you for devotion and compunction. It would be more expedient for many that they thought of the pains of Hell and the fire of Purgatory: rather than of the breadth of the world and the height of Heaven. For to think and speak of the awful judgement to come and of the punishments of the reprobate: often strikes fear, which is very profitable for the lukewarm and dissolute. But to speak of the empyreal heaven and of the nine choirs of angels, does not profit young and unmortified monks: who are easily uplifted, when they read or hear any subtle matters: it were better they were silent of these things, and examined and mourned their own shortcomings.

Brethren, then you do truly wisely if you know your own vices: and bitterly repent of all the evils which you have done. Alas, how much good you lose every hour idling and talking: which you might gain by toiling, keeping silence and praying. Purpose strongly therefore to amend and make fervent progress: and persevere with constancy in the Order. Lift up your eyes very often with humble prayer to the Lord in Heaven, groaning: and praying for your sins in the secret of your heart. Such God loves: who often lift up their hearts to heavenly things and pray. He freely forgives your past faults if you crave pardon: and seek and keep His grace. Never foolishly think great and high things of yourselves: lest you fall before you know it.

When, therefore, you think or say or do anything good: you must not attribute this to yourselves even in the least; but immediately strive to return it all, with giving of thanks, wholly to God: from Whom comes all the good that you recognize in yourselves, and see in others. All things are the gifts of God, which beautify the body and soul: for God has given being, life, feeling, action, discernment and understanding. It is a great blindness of heart, not to consider the divine gifts: and how much we are obliged to thank the Creator. So great are the blessings of God that they cannot be numbered: or sufficiently unfolded. Grievously, therefore, they sin and displease God by ingratitude: who, entangled in vanities, do not render to God devout thanks for His favours. Whence the apostle Paul saith: "Give thanks always for all things: in the name of our Lord Jesus Christ." And David singing on the Psaltery and harp: after many favours bestowed, rendering thanks to God, says: "Unto Thee, O my helper, will I sing; for Thou art God my defence: my God, my mercy." And the same Lord speaks by Isaias the prophet, saying: "I will not give My glory to another." What then shall we say to this, who do little or no good: and nevertheless desire to glory and to be praised? A base thing utterly: to wish to be esteemed for virtues which we do not possess. Let us abandon this vanity: let us follow the holy apostles and prophets, who were truly saints: and nevertheless attributed nothing of their holiness to themselves but all to God.

When, therefore, we seek the honour and glory of God, and render thanks to Him simply and wholly for all good things bestowed upon us; then we rise above with the angels in Heaven: who at the birth of Christ sang glory to God in the highest. But when we seek empty glory without of any good, or take pleasure in ourselves within, and weigh our good more than we should; then we are not truthful, nor humble in the truth, but proud and foolish: despised of God, reprobate of the angels, and strangers to all the saints. Whence from the vice of elation we fall beneath ourselves, and by degrees approach Hell; because we are likened to the demons and the damned, who do not love or praise God: nor are able to gaze upon the glory of God. And because they do not pay the honour due to God nor freely humble themselves with the saints; but perversely and proudly resist their Creator: by a just judgement of God they carry the torment of hell everywhere with them, and wither away in their malice. They are burnt by the flames, and not cleansed: they are most cruelly tortured, and never amend. From the moment they sought glory in themselves, they lost Heaven: and fell from the eternal glory of God into everlasting shame. Thus, alas, poor wretches, proud men glorying in themselves and despising others, shall speedily perish, before they are aware: who presuming of themselves say or think: "Our mighty hand: and not the Lord, hath done all these things." Be therefore, brethren, humble of heart, chaste, kind, modest, compassionate: prudent in word, diligent in toil: fervent in prayer, patient in tribulation: obedient without delay, simple without questioning: retiring without pretence, silent without suspicion: submissive without complaint.

When also God of His great loving-kindness inspires or reveals anything good to one in prayer or study: let him not at once extol himself for this, nor prefer himself to others, or deem himself more holy; but he must think and believe that God hath done this to him not on account of his own virtues and labours, nor on account of his merits and ingenious toil: but because of His immense goodness, whereby He sends down rain upon the good and the bad, pouring forth His mercy upon every creature. For thus he speaks by the prophet Ezechiel to the Jews taking pride in the good things vouchsafed them: "It is not for your sakes but for My own sake that I have done this, House of Israel: be it known to you." Let no man then abuse the divine goodness and mercy upon him by attributing anything to himself through pride: for fear that he incur at once the displeasure of God because of his thanklessness: and hear against himself the harsh sentence of the judge fearfully thundering: "Take away the pound from him, that is, the grace of devotion of which he is unworthy because of vainglory: and give to him that hath ten pounds, on account of his humility and thankfulness." For he is meet to receive greater gifts; who studies ever to return thanks to God for the lesser: and confesses himself unworthy of all. The most loving Lord often gives His consolation not only for the sake of one man or two comforting one another; but also for the sake of the edification of others, and the instruction of many to the love and praise of so pious, sweet and generous a Master in His gifts: Who is so good and beneficent in bestowing His grace upon the humble, the mild and the compunct of heart. But He soon withdraws His sweetness from the elated and thankless: from idle talkers, from the curious, from the deceitful and murmurers. For the heart must be free of vices, if the sweetness of the Holy Spirit is to enter: which is more precious than all earthly riches. And he shall be enriched with eternal good things in Heaven: who spurns to take pleasure in the praises of men. Seek, therefore, rather to be comforted in devout prayers and tears: than in deep questions and long discourses. Study in the book of the conscience: flee the shadow of vainglory: store up oil in your vessels with the wise virgins: hide the treasure of your heart in the valley of humility. For if you seek the summit of true honour: you will hasten to that heavenly fatherland with your whole desire. To the happy gaining of which: may Jesus Christ lead us all. Amen.

PART II

SERMON X

OF THE MANY TRIALS OF THE JUST FOR THE KINGDOM OF HEAVEN

MANY are the tribulations of the just: and out of them all will the Lord deliver them. Beloved brethren, look into the life of the saints; eagerly hear and read the teaching of the saints: desire to follow their examples; and constantly implore their glorious intercession, that you may be strong in adversity: and may be able to bear with constancy for Christ all the toils of the day and the night. Doubt not of the future promise of Christ: which He will render to them that love Him, when their work is accomplished and their combat bravely ended. You have not been in Hell nor in Lucifer's pit: therefore the statutes of the cloister seem burdensome to you. You have not experienced the fire of Purgatory: therefore you dread to bear the word of reproach, the strictness of silence, the hardness of your couch, the severity of the fast, the coarseness of the food: the fatigue of singing and the frequency of prayer. If you would have all things according to your fancy; what do you merit thereby before God? This is not in agreement with the saints: who suffered most grievous afflictions for many years. Consider then in your small labours and distresses, the most bitter sufferings of the martyrs; and by true virtue imitate the combat of those: whose festivals you celebrate through the year. And when you feel any trial, take up the buckler of patience: lest you fail in religion before the time for the end of the struggle. Let it not scandalize thee, if the wicked flourish in the world, and the good groan under the yoke; if the perverse rejoice in honours: and the good are deprived of necessaries and friends. God merciful and just provides better and everlasting goods for His elect, to be bestowed hereafter; whom now He strikes and chastises in divers ways by means of the wicked: that they may be made the more worthy to receive greater rewards in the heavenly kingdoms. Many therefore are the tribulations of the just: but many also are the scourges of sinners, which are the commencement of future sorrows. And who shall be able fully to ponder and fathom the abyss of the judgements of God upon the sons of men? For the Lord is just and hath loved justice; Who to the good and righteous of heart ordains all things unto good and turns all to their salvation: and to the wicked, hard, and perverse changes all unto their destruction and grief. Bear therefore, brethren, as good and faithful servants of Christ, with patient heart and willing soul, the small burdens which at times trouble you and prove how strong you are; for they will not last long nor confound the humble: but borne devoutly they will greatly rejoice your souls according to that of the Psalmist: "The bones that have been humbled shall rejoice: and He will save the humble of spirit." If we were truly humble and willing to balance strictly the weight of our sins; we should find nothing unbearable: we should say that we scarcely receive one for a thousand. For it behoved Christ to suffer, Who nevertheless did no sin: how much more us, miserable sinners, who daily in many things offend many: namely, God, the angels, the saints, and men. But God suffers many tribulations to fall upon His elect not to their reprobation; but for the cleansing of sins, for the increase of merits, for a greater warning: and for the strengthening of their weakness by the virtue of patience.

Let each then set himself to patience, if he will have peace of heart: if he wishes to receive a crown of glory in Heaven, after the toil of his combat. This temporal life is full of stones and thorns; and therein the elect are exercised and tried by hardships: that they may the more eagerly long for the eternal goods. Behold God spares no man; but gives to each his own burden to bear: that he may have occasion to merit much. For some things come and tempt us on the right by flattery: others on the left by blame; some meet us in face with a harsh countenance: others pierce us behind by the bite of detraction; some constrain us from above to labour: others froth up from below to ridicule, as the little boys with the holy Elisaeus. By these six winds the condition of the present life is buffeted: and every Christian assaulted whether religious or secular. Neither rich man nor poor, neither whole nor sickly: is without his burden. Each has enough to bear; and he who makes ready and bends his back for it: does wisely and will carry it more easily. But he who seeks to idle and amuse himself with gossip; and wander through the offices and the meadows: he shall fall among robbers and fierce dogs; that is, on various temptations of the flesh, which destroy the grace of devotion: and pierce the conscience with many wounds.

Thus is a professed religious in the cloister: as a noble warrior in camp surrounded on all sides by the enemy. He cannot fly, he cannot give way to idleness: but he must watch and stand ever to arms against the snares and arrows of his foes. For unless the soldier of Christ be girded with the girdle of chastity and defended on all sides by the shield of patience: speedily he is either disturbed, or cast down, or wounded. Stand therefore in the fear of God and prepare yourselves to fight against your passions and the vexations of men and wicked tongues; for you will always have some adversary, now this one, now that: according as God suffers to humble you lest you grow proud in good: and by vainglory lose all. But if you bear with your adversaries humbly and patiently; you shall be acceptable to God, and made like to the holy martyrs in suffering: and in the heavenly kingdom most glorious and sublime. It is utterly necessary that humility go before glory: and patience make ready with many blows the crown for the victors. For without patience and struggle and toil: vain is the hope of heavenly reward. Put you on therefore, beloved brethren, as blessed Paul saith, the breastplate of faith, doubting not of the help of God: recalling amid distresses for your supreme comfort the divine promises: and place your whole hope in God and not in men; for men often deceive and are deceived in their opinions and devices: they meditate vain things and speak foolish; they look not to the future judgements: nor fear God as they should.

Be especially on your guard against passionate men and deceitful, against dissolute and jesting companions; lest you learn to gossip and laugh with the frivolous: who walk by pleasant ways to evil hospices. But let your conversation be with the simple and humble, with the meek and devout; that from them you may receive spiritual consolation: and make more and more progress in virtue. Patience and fortitude are exceedingly necessary to you: who are in religion and stand under obedience. And so obey with a willing soul and a full heart: and strive to follow the good advice of seniors: although at times the things which they command seem hard and base. As therefore from every side assaults threaten to attack your weakness; so there are very great rewards set in the right hand of God: to be rendered to you for your much patience in all your tribulations. Encourage yourselves therefore to bear all: and cast not away the burdens which merit everlasting joys.

For from superiors it behoves you often to endure correction for your excesses: because it is better to be purged here than hereafter. But also it is most safe to obey their commands for God's sake: if you will be most happily crowned with the elect. Submit yourselves therefore freely to their ordering; that they may guide you by a safer way and a shorter distance amid so many foes and perils: to the harbour of salvation, without a murmur or any sinister suspicion.

From inferiors it behoves you to bear their defects both of conduct and of body, the which is a work of piety; and sometimes to suffer also derision: which is a sign of mildness.

On the right it behoves you to take careful heed lest you be beguiled by flattery and vain praise; lest you deem yourselves holy and just: or lift your hearts above that which is said. Often empty praise harms: soft words deceive light souls: as the snarer sweetly discoursing on his flute beguiles and captures the birds. Therefore seek not but shun honour or praise from men: lest you lose the full reward with God for foolish fables. Many praise to the face: behind the back they relate defects. He who looks into his own conscience: does not value or desire the praises of men.

On the left it behoves you to exercise great caution; that you be not troubled by those, who blame your actions, scoffing, denouncing, and giving an evil sense to the good: that you be not impatient in heart, or answer harshly in words; because perchance they wish to prove you by reproaches: whether you are truly humble and patient in adversity.

From in front it behoves you to consider with whom you speak, with whom you stand and walk: of what manner are your neighbours and comrades in their conduct, words and actions: lest haply you be seduced and infected by bad example through dissipation and licence most harmful to the young. For often after light jesting there comes the sorrow of a saddened conscience: according to the proverb of Solomon: "Mourning taketh hold of the end of joy: and laughter shall be mingled with sorrow." You must not believe every word: nor soon carry further what you have heard. For all things are not edifying: nor is it expedient to know the secrets of others. Often lies are narrated as true: which things draw the hearers away from heavenly desires. Refrain then from trifles and jests, which hinder godly pursuits; dull the understanding, distract the memory: and disturb the peaceful with unfounded suspicions.

From behind it behoves you also to keep a watchful eye; and to think not a little beforehand of perils to come: to wit, what trials might befall you through those whom now you hold as your friends. Make ready then your back to bear every issue of ill; to wash away past sins; to shun present amusements: and to lessen the future pains of Purgatory. For the reproaches, detractions, accusations and ridicule of men patiently received: are an excellent medicine for the health of the soul: justly inflicted by a most just God on sinners. The sharp reproof of words then will not harm if you are well-disposed and guiltless: for a harsh word is profitable for the correction of the dissipated.

You have now heard from the above in how many dangerous combats you are engaged, and what great good you may merit if you fight manfully. Be not therefore slack, nor lose courage because of the multitude of the enemy: but with religious anxiety strive ever to make progress unto better and more fervent practice; so that by longanimity and patience in virtues and many labours you may attain eternal repose, safe from all evils: when our Lord Jesus Christ shall bestow upon you through the intercession of His holy martyrs the crown of eternal life you have long desired. Amen.

SERMON XI

OF THE DAILY MARTYRDOM AND WARFARE IN THE RELIGIOUS STATE

ECAUSE for Thy sake we are killed all the day long: we are counted as sheep for the slaughter. Beloved brother, note well these words just read in your hearing: which long before your birth were most wholesomely uttered for your instruction by the prophet in the psalm. Blessed be God Who has called you from the present wicked world in which many are endangered soul and body: pursuing the desires of the flesh and fleeting honours. See your vocation then to this Congregation prepared by God: wherein you can merit in a short time with little labour life eternal. Behold you have entered religion, you have freely renounced your own; and in a certain manner you are dead to the world: or you should deem yourselves as dead and buried. For this your habit shows without, and the report has gone abroad of you: that you are not of the world, but all sons of God on high. For men in the world often say of religious persons: "He who serves God mocks the whole world: and he does very wisely. He assures himself of Heaven: and he has no fear of hell." Mortify therefore your members which are upon the earth: lest the envy of the devil again entice you; and drag you with him to eternal punishment through the softness of the flesh. It is certainly a great toil to struggle daily against passions and vices: but rewards exceeding great are promised to them that overcome. Think over the words which are so heartily sung in our church of the holy martyrs for their praise and as a memorial to obtain their suffrages: the sweetness of which ought to touch the depths of our heart: and arouse our lukewarmness to bear for Christ at least a few contradictions. For thus do we often recite at Vespers: "The saints of God had a mighty conflict: they passed through fire and water, and they have been saved." O beloved brethren, who stand in religion under obedience: if you faithfully fulfill what you have vowed, you are martyrs: and still you can become so by daily suffering. For so often shall you receive new crowns and precious jewels for your combat: as often as you present the different members of your body to daily labours for Christ. And if you abandon your own will, and strongly resist your sensuality: you shall receive great consolation from God within. Every religious living in obedience ready to crush his own will, and humbly endeavouring to obey his superior: he truly becomes a martyr in spirit: although he be not struck on the neck with the material sword. And whoever gives himself to perfect mortification the whole day, that is, the whole time of his life, obeying from a simple heart, he imitates Abraham: who refused not to offer as a holocaust, to bind and to slay his only beloved son Isaac. We read also of the holy martyrs that by divers kinds of torments they attained the kingdom of Heaven: who did not choose according to their own liking what species of torture or death they should suffer; but they committed themselves utterly to the divine ordering: they presented with constancy body and soul to their Creator to endure all things. When therefore any of you hears a command distasteful to him imposed by the superior, and nevertheless is ready to obey: if then also he strives to do himself violence, and restrains and stifles the rising complaint; then he offers a most agreeable sacrifice to God on the altar of his heart: and with the martyrs being made victorious over himself gloriously triumphs over the enemy. For many martyrs were violently dragged to prison, and there were bound with most cruel iron chains: yea, also were abandoned to lie without food and drink, without light and any solace from man, in filth and the fear of death. And nevertheless they remained constant in the faith of Christ, and strove to give thanks to God in their pains: for that they merited to suffer reproaches and torments for His name. Looking upon these examples do not give way in adversities, and complain of too great poverty: nor because of the severity of discipline flee from the battle before the end of the victory. They worthily merit to be crowned: who lawfully struggle and persevere. Most light is all the fatigue of our penance in comparison of the sufferings and abstinence of the holy martyrs: and in consideration of the pains of hell.

You have often heard in the torments of the martyrs, that they were tortured in divers members: and after most grievous pains were deprived of the same members, then given to most ferocious beasts to be devoured: or even thrown into burning flames. You have not yet, brethren, experienced these things: you have not yet been thus tried or proved: not yet thus tortured and beaten: not yet thus derided, or filled with reproaches: not yet driven from your houses in nakedness and shame, and publicly dragged through the streets. You have not yet resisted temptations unto the shedding of blood: nor suffered a hand or a foot to be cut off for faith and chastity. But if you often faint in the very small sufferings for Christ which befall in religion: how could you bear greater in persecution? For there are many things wherein you can try your fortitude although you shed not blood: nor resist even to the mutilation of your limbs. The holy martyrs presented their members to most grievous torments: you must chastise your body in many fastings and watches, in silence and toil, lest it grow insolent. For he who receives and endures every bitter for sweet, every coarseness for beauty, every sorrow for joy: this one truly drinks the chalice of the Lord with the martyrs; and in the sufferings to come he shall not fear to be burned: but he shall supremely rejoice to be associated in the choirs of the saints. You must choose one of these: either to burn for ever with the demons for small pleasures: or for a slight abstinence, enjoy everlasting glory with the holy angels. And because the martyrs had in mind the never-ending torments: therefore they bore easily transitory evils: and preferred to enter by the narrow way to the broad realms of Heaven. Every one in the Order living religiously and devoutly in his state, can gain the palm of martyrdom: if he struggles bravely against his vices, if he prays for his adversaries and detractors: if he earnestly keeps his chastity unspotted: if he observes obedience even unto death after the example of Christ: if he always desires to have rather less than more of all earthly things and of the necessaries of this life: if in all he seeks the good pleasure of God and forsakes his own will. holy voluntary poverty is reckoned as a martyrdom: and therefore as to martyrs so also to the poor the kingdom of Heaven is promised and given by the Lord. When therefore silence is enjoined on one talkative and dissolute, that he speak not to outsiders or to a brother; then the tongue prone to gossip is bound as by a cord: and curbed in silence that it harm not another. And indeed it is better for many that are wordy modestly to keep silence for peace of conscience: rather than from here and there piece together stories of life in the world. And when to a restless man word is given to remain in the cloister, or to dwell quietly in his cell: then his feet by a pious violence are set as it were in the stocks; and thus the fickle heart is compelled to return to the way of salvation: according to that word of the Lord: "Go out quickly into the streets and lanes of the city: and compel them to come in." Alas, how many by wandering abroad have perished: how many obeying their curiosity have added nothing to their holiness. O how many have been brought back by the rod of the superior to the keeping of their conscience and a good life: and have made a virtue of necessity. When the curious man closes his eyes, that he may not behold the vanities of the world: then he receives a reward with the saints: whose eyes were blinded by tyrants. When an idler is forced to toil: then he is dragged by hands and feet to the place of martyrdom; and if he obeys in all that is enjoined him: he shall be recompensed with the martyrs whose hands were fettered with chains, and whose feet were hung in the rack. The good obedient brother then ought to reflect that he has not command over his own body, but the superior: to whom he has freely resigned himself for God's sake: to go and do what he shall order for the salvation of his soul. For thus shall he gain the palm of patience with the martyrs: and the crown of life eternal. By the gift of our Lord Jesus Christ, Who reigneth for ever and ever. Amen.

SERMON XII

OF THE WISDOM OF CONFESSORS AND THE CONTINENCE OF RELIGIOUS

THE mouth of the just shall meditate wisdom: and his tongue shall speak judgement. Beloved brethren, these words are wont to be chanted of Confessors and Doctors: whom we ought to honour with a special devotion, and earnestly implore their suffrages: that strenuously imitating their virtues, we may merit after the course of the present life is accomplished to attain their fellowship. Therefore if we cannot bear most grievous and varied kinds of tortures with the holy martrys; let us endeavour in the measure of our strength to live in holy religion, humbly, patiently, and continently with the Confessors and Hermits: as they also pleased God, macerating the flesh by many long watchings and fasts. For the prophet in the verse of the psalm quoted describes, what is the manner of life of the just man who is pleasing to God: and how happy is his end, who shall have remained steadfast in his holy purpose. For the life of the just man and the good religious is usually remarked, and especially praised for certain characteristics; to wit, that he have his mouth shut against evil, his tongue learned in good: his heart at rest from disturbance, devout in prayer, suspended in contemplation: that he do good work with a right intention towards God: and that he be without evil suspicion towards his neighbour. And who desires to have these things, let him set the law of God in his heart: let him often meditate, willingly hear and read the sacred words: but of worldly things be silent, only of those things that belong to the salvation of the soul take the fullest care: cast away anxieties that do not concern him, indulge no time in idleness; but either pray, or study, or toil: that thereby he may be able as a faithful servant daily to increase the talent of good work. Let him learn before he teaches; and choose rather to be silent than to speak: if he wishes to become wise. Let his words be few and profitable: let him utter each with modesty: let him shun appearing before the great: let him arrange all his actions and discourses with the fear of God: as to be judged by Him, if he offend in aught. It is safer therefore and better that a man hold his peace: who knows not how to speak duly. If any inexperienced desire to have divine wisdom, let him spurn the delights of the flesh, let him keep strict watch over his outward senses, lest he drink in the vanities of the world: let him turn himself to inner things, let him examine his shortcomings: let him search his conscience every day, lament his guilt, leave naught unpunished; sigh for the things of Heaven, fear the judgement to come: deem the present life a prison, feel it a penalty to be away from Christ; consider it a great sorrow not to be assisting in the choirs of the saints: covet to possess nothing in this world, that he may have a heart ever free: esteem all temporal joy mourning: and for the desire of eternity reckon all plenty of goods poverty. The dissipated and talkative man knows not these interior sentiments: and he who ambitions honours: shall never find true wisdom. Blessed therefore that religious in whose heart the law of God reposes: whose mouth meditates the wisdom of the saints, not the folly of the world: whose learned tongue treats right judgement in every case, lest it utter anything in vain as to the wind; whose good works ever aim at the good-pleasure of God: whose steps within and without are ever directed in accordance with the divine teaching. It belongs therefore to a wise and spiritual man to discern the true from the false: vice from virtue, the necessary from the superfluous, the honourable from the scandalous: the bright from the dark, the expedient from the unlawful, the private from the public: the twisted from the upright, the just from the perverse, and the simple from the cunning: the innocent from the feigned and deceitful. Whence the Lord by the prophet Jeremias says in praise of the just man: "If thou shalt separate the precious from the vile: thou shalt be as My mouth." God is truthful and just, and He hath loved justice: His countenance hath beheld righteousness. And therefore He seeks and loves such: as walk before Him in truth. Their steps shall not be supplanted by the adversary the devil; nor by the flatteries of the world, nor by their own concupiscences: nor are they seduced by the praise or the blame of others. For the right hand of God guards under His wing them that walk in simplicity of heart: and all that they say and do shall profit them unto very great merit, and an everlasting reward. Which when they have happily attained: there will be naught for them to desire further. For blessed are all, who shall be worthy to be present in the kingdom of God and to feast and rejoice with Christ; for that they have loved Christ in their life: and have reckoned as base all earthly things.

Beloved brethren, imitate the humble life of Jesus Christ, as also did the holy Confessors: among whom were many noble and wealthy men, who long led a life truly godly and austere in abstinence from meats, in want of wheat, wine and oil and other pleasant foods: crucifying their weak flesh with its vices and concupiscences, not for the sake of the praise of men: but to satisfy unto God for their sins by fervent penance. These striving against the temptations of the devil and the honours of the world unto death: at length accomplished the course of their life in a happy end. Although therefore these did not endure in their body the sword of tyrants, or burning fire, or the tearing of beasts, or other dreadful torments: nevertheless they waged a most mighty warfare and a daily martyrdom in their spirit; embracing in preference to all the treasures of the world a life chaste, humble, lowly, interior, devout, kind, patient, sober, modest, poor and hidden: and therefore they worthily merited to have eternal crowns. If therefore you seek true wisdom, and desire to possess a peaceful life pleasing to God and agreeable to men, then give yourselves to true humility of heart, as it is written: "Where humility is: there is wisdom." This wisdom the world hates, the devil attacks; the flesh abhors, the fool derides: the proud man spurns, the passionate persecutes. For a humble and chaste life is more pleasing to God: than deep knowledge: and a good and pure conscience is more to be desired: than subtle and wordy eloquence. Simple obedience also is much better: than a clever excuse of the mouth. The keeping of silence is more profitable: than extorted permission to speak. For God protects the simply obedient: and He often suffers the cunning to come to a foolish end. It is no small prudence, to give heed to oneself: and to humble oneself under every creature: for God humbled Himself for man even to the lowest degree of earth, that He might convert sinners: and draw the penitent by true humility to the heights of Heaven, and make them blessed for ever. Many learned philosophers and great in their own eyes, have neglected the path of saving prudence, or have not known it: and departing from the humility of Christ have wandered from the truth: and have hardly been able to attain contempt of the world. Many masters also drawing the science of God and the knowledge of the virtues from long study, preach excellently well of humility and chastity, of contempt of the world and holy religion and obedience; who nevertheless held back by the love of the world barely follow Christ from afar: and, as the saying goes, do not attempt to touch with a finger the burden which they praise. So noble a virtue is humility: that often the proud and worldlings praise it. And so laudable is the virtue of chastity; that even the incontinent grandly extol it: and to their own shame honour it with meet praise. And this certainly is from God: Who glorifies His most faithful lovers and chaste and humble servants in the present where they are strangers and pilgrims; whom in the dwelling of the blessedness to come, He intends to rejoice with a fuller glory for all the confusion which they have endured. Whoever then lives continently, and keeps his senses under the regular discipline within and without; he shall be justly called a Confessor of the Lord: because he was prudent and faithful over a few goods. For of the five talents delivered to him, that is, the five senses of his body, he was a good steward: living blamelessly, and showing others a good example. For these two things especially in religious and retired persons please God, and shine before men: a good life and holy doctrine. And such a servant after his labours have been accomplished shall enter gladly into the joy of his Lord: because he was found faithful in every work and good word: to the praise of God and the edification of the neighbour for ever and ever. Amen.

SERMON XIII

OF A CAREFUL WATCH OVER THE HEART, AND THE GRACE OF INTERIOR DEVOTION

WITH all watchfulness keep thy heart: because life issueth out from it. Beloved brethren, carefully ponder the admonition of the most wise king Solomon: and anxiously watch over the keeping of your heart: lest the devil find an opening to enter. He does not seek aught but to deceive you: and guilefully to draw you away from God. For when the heart of man is withdrawn from the sovereign good; then it seems to be delighted in the lowest: and is driven hither and thither by various desires. And he who does not withstand betimes: is taken captive and overcome. Nothing is more toilsome than to guard the heart from wandering and from vicious imaginations: gathered from the things of sense. The heart of man is perverse and unsearchable; and prone to evil from his youth. And who can know it; and reckon all its motions every day? Certainly God alone, Who beholds all things before they happen: of Whom it is said in the Psalm: "The Lord knoweth the thoughts of men: that they are vain." The heart is never at rest from occupation in something: whether it be good or evil. In good the heart is comforted: in evil it is troubled. If any man desire to keep his heart and to restrain it from wandering; let him endeavour to take up a good meditation; and gather honeycomb from the words of Holy Writ, whereby to nourish his soul: let him dismiss light words, not seek curious things; not uplift himself in prosperity; in adversity keep patience: and freely commit to God all things that are to come upon him. Let him also especially ponder this, how he can possess union with God: Who seeks a dwelling-place in a reposeful heart. Therefore with all his strength let him separate himself from lower cares: and by inflamed prayers and frequent sighs raise up his heart wont to wander, and say: "My eyes are ever towards the Lord." And as often as from frailty, or some need he be hindered from the supreme good: let him begin afresh, and speedily rise by prayer; repent with groans and sorrow that for a moment he neglected the Creator for the creature: to Whom according to his powers he ought to aspire with all his affections and constantly cleave. For from holy reading is drawn a good meditation about God: from a good meditation proceeds devout affection and ready raising of the mind to God. Thence arises fervent and interior prayer piercing the heavens: forsaking all creatures, and longing to cleave to God alone: in Whom are all good things that can be desired. For God alone it is Who fills the whole desire of the soul, pacifies, and rejoices; to Whom every religious should aspire and fly, loving secrecy: and shunning occasions of discourse. For he who seeks places to wander abroad, and neglects to watch over his heart: either does not relish this grace of union: or tasting it but little speedily loses it. And, alas, hardly with great labour and sorrow shall he recover the sweetness of devotion: because he did not keep it with sufficient care. It remains then, leaving aside all trifles, earnestly to flee to Christ and to be united in friendship chiefly with Him: and to cast away and reject all things that withdraw from His love. Whatever does not make a good conscience, or give or increase the heat of the love of Christ; is utterly to be shunned and refused by every cloistered man and religious monk: whose heart ought to be in Heaven, not wandering in the world. O brother monk, who bearest the appearance of holiness in habit and name: close the door of thy mouth and show not the secret of thy heart to all. Open the chamber of thy heart to Jesus Christ the most loving comforter and the most faithful protector of thy life; so that the blessed Jesus before all and above all in Heaven and on earth beloved of thee, long desired and awaited: may deign to come to thee, and take up His abode. Earnestly beseech that He often visit thee and illumine: teach thy ignorance, strengthen thy cowardice; upraise thy heart, drive away distrust: strengthen thy faith, pour in love, and increase fervour. O how well he is guarded and armed against the snares of the devil and evil thoughts and impure imaginations, who has the image of the Crucified fixed in his heart, penetrating all his interior: and always and everywhere urging to the thought and performance of every good. Then inwardly consoled with wondrous sweetness of heart from the presence of Christ shall he be able justly to say: what holy David with great joy sang to God: "I have run the way of Thy commandments: when Thou didst enlarge my heart." Let nothing then come between thee and Jesus, the lover of innocence and purity, nor lie concealed within, nor endure: yea not even touch as in passing, nor caress with vain praises lest it infect: for the pure and tender heart offered to God in religion: does not suffer with Him anyone outside of Jesus to be joined or converse with it. For all things comforting and beautiful for a time in creatures do not suffice for the full joy of the soul: but Jesus alone is able to satisfy every desire. All things out of Jesus crucified beget weariness and fall short: and as absinthe and most bitter gall torment the soul occupied with various desires. The source therefore of all good and the honeyed stream of all consolation: is Jesus Christ, the true comforter of souls. He who wishes to be comforted by God, let him choose Jesus as his companion: with Whom to speak and walk until he arrive in Heaven. Strive to live in the love of Jesus, to die to the whole world: and to glory in the cross of Christ, not in thyself, or in men. That hour is to be often considered by thee: when thou shalt not be able to utter another word, or move a limb. And although the religious be deprived of earthly goods and friends: he has nevertheless a heavenly treasure locked up in the casket of his heart, Jesus Christ and Him crucified. He has also a most faithful friend of his soul and a most wise guide of his life: the very King of angels and Creator of all things. Wilt thou then have peace and tranquillity of heart: and merit the grace of Christ and the friendship of the angels? Despise thyself for Christ: and as much as is possible aim to have a heart pure, cut off from the world: fervent to things divine and uplifted to heavenly things. For he who seeks no earthly solace without: loves naught in creatures unduly: shall speedily experience interior peace and the love of Christ: and shall most easily bear with the comfort and aid of Christ within all burdens whencesoever they come. For he cuts off many occasions of trouble: he escapes and overcomes many snares of temptations: who for Christ's sake perfectly strips and separates himself from all earthly desires. This man, oppressed by no weight of earthly things, can freely fly to heavenly things: as often as he shall be mindful of his dear lover, Who is in Heaven: or shall hear or read His words. Sadness indeed for the absence of Jesus sharply pierces; but love from the presence of His grace soothes the languishing soul: consoles the sorrowful, and enkindles the lukewarm. He who cannot so quickly attain this grace of devotion and height of contemplation: let him not lose courage, nor cease to labour: let him groan, pray, sit apart: be silent and recollect himself, await with longanimity, hope with confidence: and he shall be abundantly consoled beyond all that can be thought. For Jesus is loving towards all His saints: and He abandons not them that hope in Him. He frequently proves, He lovingly corrects, He wisely instructs; He calls incessantly, He knocks loudly, He opens freely, He receives joyously: He pardons tenderly, He gives abundantly, He crowns gloriously. Let not therefore the loving blows of Jesus crush thee; and disdain not to listen to His sacred words: by whomsoever or wheresoever they be read. Let not the inconstancy of thy heart cast thee down, nor sickness of body: nor aching of head, incurred in the service of Christ. He Who created thee and called thee to His service: will not be wanting to thee in thy suffering for His name. For all the ills which thou endurest, and whatever good thou shalt do in this house to the honour of God persevering in discipline; shall be written in the book of eternal life: and shall be accounted to thee for a very great reward in the kingdom of Heaven. Turn thee then away from vain things, return to the interior of the mind; think over the benefits of thy dear Lover often vouchsafed to thee: and the still greater to be made known in the time to come. Let His boundless loving-kindness draw thee gratefully to serve the most gentle Saviour: His infinite goodness to love Him: His charity, enduring unto all time, to hope in His mercy: promised to the truly penitent in the end, to be rendered to them that persevere. All things pass away except the love of God; all things perish without Christ: all things become bitter without Jesus incarnate, suffering, crucified, risen, and glorified for the salvation of the world. Let this be your wisdom, brethren, choose this as your study in preference to all study of letters: to meditate day and night on Jesus crucified, sacrificed for us all on the cross, and exalted in Heaven: so that your whole hope tend upwards unto Him lovable and praiseworthy above all. Therefore to suffer for Him and to be wearied in His service: reckon a very great treasure found in the field of the holy cross. Meditation on the divine works and words of Christ begets sweetness and joy: strengthens faith, raises hope, and enkindles charity in the heart: which He has promised that He will give to His faithful. But the devil in envy, who dared to tempt Christ, and has often aroused persecutions in the Church, and afflicted many of the saints: still does not cease molesting the devout: inducing weariness of good, and dissuading from the severity of the cloister. Alas, with his cunning suggestion he beguiles many by softness and caresses: he terrifies by hardships and austerities. However with the help of Christ his most wicked darts shall not harm: but they shall be to them that fight bravely and resist manfully unto praise and glory: and to the devil unto everlasting shame and punishment. From whose snares and frauds may Jesus Christ ever defend us: Who is at the right hand of the Father above all, God blessed for ever. Amen.

RELIGIOUS, NOTE

Said a certain devout lover of solitude. "Blessed is the lonely monk: to whom the world is an exile, Heaven a fatherland: the cell Paradise. Blessed the religious, devout to God, unknown to the world: to whom the town is a prison, the cloister a place of refreshment: toil repose, solitude solace: mourning joy, silence the asylum of peace. Blessed he to whom sacred reading is food: prayer drink, psalmody recreation: meditation Christ, contemplation God. Blessed the religious who directs all his pursuits and exercises to virtue and the good-pleasure of God: and aims at nothing singular and showy in word or deed: everywhere careful not to give offence to God or the neighbour. Blessed he who takes it in good part when one corrects him and teaches him aright: lest he abide in error and perish miserably. Blessed he who strictly guards his mouth: that he utter not an idle or hurtful word. Such a one shall have great peace, a good conscience and repute: and shall gain a special grace of devotion. He makes many quarrels cease: who is patient and holds his peace. The religious abiding in retirement: is as a lamp in the night safely burning. Winds have blown: and they shall not harm him who takes leisure in God and prays. There is truly a great treasure in the mouth of the wise man: but not a less in the heart of him that is silent and prays." A certain man of experience said: "Whatever good I gather by silence: I scatter it nearly all by talking with men." Because Samson told his secret to a woman, and did not conceal the parable of the honey: afterwards he was captured by the enemy and mocked. It is good therefore for a religious to keep silence: and carefully to weigh his words. For he who keeps silence well: as it were carries with him a bag full of money to the home of his mind.

AN EXAMPLE OF SILENCE

There was in the up-country a certain monk of the Cistercian Order, a diligent warden of his mouth: and a careful observer of cloistral discipline. He, on fire with the zeal of devotion, scarcely spoke a single word in a week. To whom the Abbot said by way of solace: "Brother, I give thee leave to speak sometimes with the brethren:" Who replied: "Reverend Father, I do not wish to have such a leave." Hearing which the Abbot was edified in the answer of the brother who so willingly kept silence.

AN EXAMPLE OF SOLITUDE

A certain brother of the Order of Regulars having been sent abroad, when he had finished his business strove to return quickly and with eagerness: that he might take leisure in God more freely in silence. But while on the way, he met a certain traveller, a friend and acquaintance of his: who stated that he had visited different holy places and monasteries. Questioned therefore concerning religious houses: he also said that he had been in the holy cloister of Chartreux. And when he had spoken much in praise of the situation of that place on a high mountain and in a lonely wilderness, and of the austerity of the brethren dwelling there: finally he narrated this: "I found there a brother, with whom it gave me great pleasure to speak: and I questioned him with curiosity, saying: 'How long hast thou dwelt here?' Who answered: 'Forty years have passed, and meanwhile I have not seen the front gate: by which I entered.' " Hearing this the aforesaid brother wondered: and related these things to his other brothers as a good example of the love of solitude. O how rare and strange is such conduct in many religious of these days; who would look on it as the penalty of a gaol: if within a year they should not go forth for the sake of travelling outside the monastic bounds, or beyond the gate.

SERMON XIV

OF CONSTANCY AND PERSEVERANCE IN THE STATE OF RELIGION

STAND with confidence: and you shall see the help of the Lord over you. Beloved brethren, accept with pleasure a word of pious exhortation urging you to perseverance in the state of religion: which has a very great recompense in Heaven. Purpose firmly in your hearts that you desire to remain with constancy in this place and Order which you have freely chosen: and to endure good things and evil with all in this house gathered together for Christ's sake long before your time. He Who has granted a good beginning: will give by His grace a better consummation. For you have not been called to this community because of your merits: but you should believe that you are made partakers of their crowns. Be glad to be aided by their prayers and to be sustained by their help: and ever give thanks to God. For you have not come to idle and feast: but to serve God with fidelity and devotion. And so much the more careful and ready should you be for every observance of the Order and for the common labours; the more advantages you now have in buildings and books, in food and clothing: which many of the elders before you had not. You have entered into their labours, be grateful therefore for the good things you have received. These temporal things made ready by God: are bestowed upon you as a present for the sustenance of your body. If you use them moderately with giving of thanks and good will; then still greater goods will be added to you in Heaven: which shall be most assuredly rendered to all who persevere in the discipline of the Order. And if you cannot yet understand or grasp the joys to come prepared in the heavenly nuptials; nevertheless firmly believe that God is faithful and mighty to give what He has promised to them that love Him: who not by force but with a free mind serve Him day and night without complaint. Therefore with great care cast out of your heart speedily harmful sadness, and all indignation as poison of the devil: and strive to live among your brethren like angels of peace among their fellow citizens. Take upon your shoulders the yoke of the Lord, light and sweet to them that love: until you attain the fatherland of everlasting bliss. But meanwhile you must be tried after the manner of the saints by divers temptations which often happen in religion: and are wont grievously to afflict novices from this side and that: that thereby proved as gold in the furnace, and purged from the rust of past bad habits: you may be bright in the sight of God as new lambs washed in the springs. For after tears and griefs you shall receive divine consolations and lights of the understanding: relieving all toil and distress. What more do you desire? Behold, now are given to you earthly goods for the support of the body on the way; and hereafter will be given heavenly and everlasting goods in the kingdom of God with the holy angels; because you have forsaken acquaintance and friends, and have chosen to serve God rather than the world. If therefore you abide constant in what you have commenced: you shall hear with joy and assurance from Christ in the judgement. "You are they who have continued with Me in My temptations; and I dispose to you, as My Father hath disposed to Me, a kingdom: that you may eat and drink at My table in My kingdom." O sweet and comforting word, encouraging to perseverance in the Order we have taken: and in whatsoever temptation and tribulation or weakness a man may be involved. It belongs certainly to God to aid: and to free the afflicted from every distress of mind and body. And he who trusts in God, praying and patiently enduring himself: he shall be comforted in due time, giving thanks for the help vouchsafed him from Heaven. God is not a respecter of persons, but in every condition and place, where there is the memory of His name under Heaven: He shall be nigh the tempted and troubled of heart. He shall hear them for His mercy; and shall show them in secret His judgements: and His wonders in all things which He works upon earth. No man can say to God, "Why dost Thou thus afflict me and leave me dry; and dost thus advance another and allow him to have many of his wishes?" Foolish and vain is this thought: even in the least thing to doubt or complain of the providence and goodness of God. It is the habit of the weak and unwise to blame and interpret ill the actions of the prudent which they do not understand; who very often wonder and are scandalized within themselves: why God suffers this or that, so evidently evil, to happen. To whom the psalmist thus replies: "The Lord is just in all His ways: and holy in all His works." And again: "Thou art just, O Lord: and Thy judgement is right." Hold this then firmly, that in every place the eyes of the Lord behold the good and the bad; and no man can hide from His judgements, nor excuse his sins with many fair words: nor appeal in contention to a higher judge. Whoever therefore abiding in a lowly condition and in his Order shall have more resolutely struggled against temptations and his vices; he shall deserve greater grace of devotion now: and hereafter shall enjoy the blessedness of a fuller glory. Every religious can save his soul and make progress in virtue in his Order and in the place provided for him by God: if he carefully observe what the Order hath established, and what the superior commands and counsels to be done. Let no one therefore be lightly seduced; nor think with foolish and vain imaginings of another place: and prophesying of the uncertain future more pleasant things to himself, say: "O God, if I were in such a place and Order: how well and devoutly I would conduct myself: and no longer complain or be troubled by anyone." Alas, miserable and foolish man, who for want of fervour dost contemplate the world outside: and often dost imagine vain things because of the distress of thy present passion; why dost thou not do this good in this place, where with the grace of many brethren, and the peace of a good conscience thou canst live with God as witness and aider? Why dost thou neglect the little things told thee; and presumest of greater things in the future? Know beforehand that it most usually befalls lukewarm and indocile disciples: otherwise and far worse than they in their mind first imagined, without fruit of any worth. This fancy has deceived many; easy changing of place has made many learned to err: hasty migration to another Order has saddened very many. For it has been very often proved in others: that seldom has he come back better, who sought many places. For wherever a man may be, he shall find men: the blind also and the weak whom certainly it behoves to bear. And haply thou wilt see some more imperfect who will not be pleasing to thee in many things: nor wilt thou likewise be pleasing to them. Some maybe will say or think of thee askance: if thou hadst been worth anything, thou wouldst rather have remained in thy place and Order with peace. However the motive of one wandering from place to place will speedily be made clear: what moved him more. For feigned holiness cannot remain concealed long, nor frivolity of soul: nor does too great freedom in wandering edify others. For the nurse of true devotion is the solitary and enclosed religious. Hear the parable of a certain devout old man. "When a man goes out lame of one foot or deprived of one eye: he seldom comes back sound in both." The fox leaving its hole: cannot long travel the high road. So a man of fickle mind and deceitful cannot long disguise himself: but he betrays himself even unwillingly before many strangers: either by manifest words or deeds. Often also a movement of anger will show the asperity of his impatience; when he is reproved for his fault: or compelled to keep silence. A proud man inwardly passionate, for a while sometimes represses himself before others: lest he be outwardly blamed and lose respect. But becoming more free in course of time: he shamelessly returns to his wont. And thus it shall be made manifest to many, that he was not truly humble: but wished to seem good and just. The temptation of the devil does not suffer a runaway to be hidden long or to live in peace; but he commences to annoy him by fresh and unexpected obstacles; and toils to vex and confound the coward in a much worse fashion: because he foolishly left his little nest. For the yoke of the Order day and night laid upon the neck of the monk: soon shows how much he can carry and endure for the love of God. Therefore in every place and condition, in every office and spiritual dignity, or temporal occupation: extremely needful is long-suffering patience and an abundant outpouring of divine grace with frequent instance in prayer; lest the weak mind, battered by frequent blows, be moved by sudden anger to impatience, or by the suggestion of Satan seek to return vengeance: bearing indignantly the insults put upon it.

Soldier of Christ, do not fly: do not cast thyself down; grow not lukewarm from thy first fervour: nor doubt of the consolation of divine sweetness. Seek not outward comforts of the body very harmful to thy soul: but for God's sake bear temptations and the vexations of men as well in this place as in another house. Nor deem thyself forsaken of God if many things befall to try thy patience; for thou art not better than Christ Who suffered: nor more holy than the martyrs who were cruelly put to death. Men act and often speak ill like men; nor is it always true what they say: nor must one care much whether they praise or blame. In all times and places beware of evil deeds and scandal: and God shall free thee from the ill word lyingly spoken of thee. It is written in one of the collects super populum of Lent. "Protect, O Lord, Thy people, and mercifully cleanse it of all sins; for no adversity shall harm it: if no wickedness overmaster it." For punishment does not make a man guilty: but guilt demands a just penalty. Have God therefore before thy eyes, neglect not to pray in trouble; write or read in due time the holy Scriptures: the better to overcome weariness of heart. God often gives in one hour: that which He has refused a whole week. Never presume of thy virtue and justice; but trust utterly in the mercy and goodness of God: and prudently and discreetly go forward between hope and despair. Never be so joyous and secure: as to shut out from thee fear and modesty. He who wishes to please God and edify the neighbour; ought so to order all his words and habits without and within: as if he were immediately to be presented before God and His angels. Do not therefore, religious brother, if thou art light and dissipated and wordy, boast of thy outward habit before men as if thou wert a saint: nor take pride in any work private or common; but rather thou shalt deem thyself unprofitable, if thou thinkest rightly: as one who canst hardly return one from a thousand talents.

Thou art not therefore to be called a holy and great master because outwardly thou wearest the cappa; which an ass might do, if he were so clothed. Heed rather the stains of thy conscience than the esteem of men; for all things are not so sound and bright before God: as they appear to be fair to men. Man sees in the face, but God in the heart; Who also considers things most minute: which thou dost not know, or weighest but little. Therefore bow down thy heart under the severe scrutiny of God; and be not vainly puffed up because of the dignity of religion: nor speak boastfully of the virtues of others and the miracles of holy men. He blackens and shames himself, who praises the holiness of his fathers: and neglects to follow their humble life; who is called a regular and a religious: and does not fervently pursue the rule of life which the saints have left to their posterity; who daily lives on the goods of the monastery: and luke warmly observes the monastic statutes, or lightly breaks them. Nevertheless on account of the holy fathers of previous days who founded the Order of religion and drew up rules of life: the slothful and dissipated also are honoured by people and magnates of the world who think them to be servants of God. Therefore let each rightly examine himself, and give others a good example: lest he do an injury to the holy Order: and beget shame to himself by his ill conduct. "Wo to that man," saith the Lord, "by whom scandal cometh." If you wish truly to know and commend any religious; look not to the white or black habit of the body, nor heed subtlety of words: but consider his humble ways, expressing the image of the interior man. Silently also reverence the grace of Christ, which he has received, and love and praise God for His gifts: Who chose for Himself such a servant in a desert land full of temptations and dangers. Cautiously however and moderately praise him whom thou lovest: lest thou deceive thyself and him: if thou say anything, beyond what is befitting, of which thou shouldst afterwards blush.

Brothers, we are all one in Christ, we have one heavenly Father: we are all called the sons of one holy mother Church, whoever believe in Christ and are baptized in Christ: therefore we ought not to dispute about the outward habit, and different manner of life; but let each study to live well in his Order and condition: and wholly to please God worthily with giving of thanks. For not agreeableness or magnitude of place, nor fair raiment, nor excellence of grace maketh a perfect religious; but utter renunciation of the world, and daily mortification of vices: and especially purity of heart, and love of virtue aiming directly at God. The name of religion has great praise among men of the world: but without contempt of the world it is of little weight with God. But what worth a noble name without virtuous deed; what profit a sublime state without humility and charity? He is truly a religious who freely renounces the world, and in his heart does not veer round again to the world; who binds himself for ever to God: and endeavours to crush all his own wishes for God's sake. For he who with the holy habit and good name thus fulfills the acts of virtue without: and yet in every thought and deed aims only at pleasing God within: he is duly to be praised and called the friend of God. If thou desirest to overcome vainglory; give heed to each of thy shortcomings as something known to all: and the movement of vainglory will cease. Beware of showing singularity in speech or conduct; do not presume too much of thyself when prosperity befalls thee: lest thou be cast down by an assault of adversity. Stay in thy place and set thyself to patience; and thou shalt find peace and grace in the sight of God and men: and thou shalt be dear to all the brethren. But that no one may easily think of changing his habit or place: I will relate you what happened to a certain brother for your greater warning.

AN EXAMPLE

There was a certain brother who had lived long respected in the Order of Regulars: and being appointed procurator gained repute and esteem with many religious and seculars. For a long time he had the temptation and desire to pass to another Order and a place remote: which also he did, but without sufficient foresight and prudence. For from the miserable issue: was afterwards made apparent the inconstancy of his mind. However he had secured for himself in secret a place with certain mendicant religious of sufficiently good observance, living under the rule of blessed Augustine: by whom also he was kindly and willingly received. Nor was there long delay in probation: but to satisfy his urgent desire he was clothed in haste. So eagerly did he seek and pant after that Order: that he would willingly have made his profession the same day: if that had pleased the brethren. But the brethren, more cautious than he, because they knew not his character and conduct: did not give way to his impatient desire: but willingly gave him the usual time of probation. For they judged according to outward appearances: that this stranger would be useful to them, for they needed persons for the reformation of the Order. But when he had been now clothed: his heart was changed to other than he had thought. And he began to be exceedingly sad and sorry: that he had left the former house where he lived so long: nnd without due cause had secretly forsaken his brethren: whom he grieved and shamed not a little by his departure. Scarcely a week had passed: and for trouble of mind he mourned and lamented so much: that he could neither eat nor drink. Questioned therefore what disturbed him: he said, "I can have no rest at all, or peace of conscience: if I do not return again to my former brethren." Hearing which the brothers were much saddened and perturbed; and they bitterly reproached his inconstancy: that in so short a time he had changed again, and had been guilty of childish presumption. To whom he replying with humility and shame: thus excused himself. "Believe me, brothers, that now for many years I have had this temptation, to cross over to another Order: and this idea was so strongly fixed in my soul: that I thought I could never change. But now I have proved by my own experience that it is otherwise: the which before I could not entertain." When therefore he had said this: that the scandal still secret might not break out and grow: having wisely consulted together, they sent to a certain Prior of the Regulars dwelling in the neighbourhood: asking him to deign to come to them with all speed, for a very urgent case of necessity. When he arrives, they explain the whole matter to him in order: and earnestly demand what is now to be done. Nor is there any delay in settling the matter, but each party contributes to the re-establishment of peace. The aforesaid brother then, repentant with great sorrow, is stripped of the habit which he had taken; and is again clothed by the Prior in the habit of Regulars in the Order to which he was accustomed: and thus the occasion of disturbance is removed and destroyed. Then a companion was given him and he returned to his former cloister; and humbly beseeching forgiveness for the offences he had committed: he was received with compassion by his brethren. And at once he received a wholesome penance: and was chastised for the error of his presumption. And rendered more cautious for the future, he learnt not to do anything rashly; and not foolishly to run to other houses.

SERMON XV

OF CAREFUL WATCHFULNESS OF THE YOUNG AGAINST MANY TEMPTATIONS

SEE how you walk circumspectly: because the days are evil. Beloved brethren, in these words the glorious teacher, blessed Paul the apostle, warns us all: to be circumspect, and to fight bravely against vices in this house of the Lord, which is the dwelling of many wayfarers of the world; wherein is raised the standard of the holy cross: as a sign of spiritual warfare for the gaining of golden crowns in the heavenly kingdoms. Wherefore let no man grow weary of the desire of progress: the Lord of armies is with us: Who is the mighty uprooter of vices and the terror of our foes. Let no man be disturbed, or affrighted, by the assault of divers temptations, or by the multitude of contrary winds: or by the fatigue of daily labours; by many tribulations we must all enter the kingdom of Heaven: the gospel of Christ preaches, and the Acts of the Apostle teach. Yea, also, the apostle Paul himself, the vessel of election, frequently rapt to the secrets of Heaven, had temptations; suffered many annoyances from men, and wearied in many toils often heard and bore detractions and unjust complaints against himself. And yet he did not because of the afflictions of adversity depart from the service and love of Christ, nor grow cold: but rather manfully offered himself to endure all; and encouraged others with him to the combat for the crown of glory: which Christ has promised to His servants who endure many contradictions for Him. And blessed Paul became so much the more joyous and assured of receiving future rewards in Heaven: the more cruelly he suffered from men known and unknown as a man contemptible in the world.

Brethren, be not too much afraid of suffering and being despised for Christ; all these things are nothing and shall speedily be ended: yea, in comparison of the good and the evil things to come, they are to be accounted as scarcely of a single point, or moment. Know then that this life and regular discipline, which by the inspiration of God you have taken up, is good, and very wholesome for your soul: but not safe from the snares of the enemy: nor always at peace from the annoyances of men and the reproaches of the perverse. For now this one, now that one says or does something: which will not be pleasing in your eyes. What then shall you do? Be patient and hold your peace; God will fight for you: and the truth will make you free. Do not lose your merit, but with silence endure a little: deeming yourselves worthy of all confusion. As yet you are not in Heaven with the holy angels; but in the world with men good and bad: who shall not be wanting in this region of the shadow of death. Therefore you may well more often lament and not lightly laugh: but rather fear and not foolishly presume of yourselves. Carefully therefore in every place and time walk in the sight of God: because you are uncertain of a good end: and how God will judge your actions you know not. "Fear the Lord, all ye His saints," saith holy David, "for there is no want to them that fear Him." Why does he urge all to fear; and to stand with great watchfulness of discipline? Because terrible are the judgements of God upon the sons of men: and no one is certain whether he is worthy of hatred or love. Therefore it is very profitable for a man still carnal, dissolute and unmortified to have the fear of God: and to fear all His works, and to think lowlily of himself. For the fear of God makes a man withdraw from sin: be on the watch against the dangers of temptations: grieve over past evils, abstain from present delights: take moderately of the necessaries of life: and rule his actions with discretion: always to aim at the more perfect: and ever to seek and diligently execute all things which please God more: and praiseworthily to draw and move all good things to the honour of His name.

Alas, alas, brethren, many perils surround us on all sides: as the flesh, the devil, and the whole world seated in wickedness. Hence are begotten dangers and temptations: and few are they who escape without wound and stain. What wonder then if a man fear for his weakness; when on all sides he sees the snares of the devil laid out for him? For if he does good, if he reads, sings or writes well: if he prays, studies, preaches, or celebrates; behold at once the devil is there with vainglory, attacking the just man by means of success: desiring to cast him down, and to deprive him of the grace bestowed on him by God. But if he fall into any fault through frailty: at once the foe runs up with joy: and suggests that it is not a great evil, nor seriously to be punished, but even to be confessed shortly and carefully excused: since many do and have done the like and worse. Thus the cunning adversary beguiles him who has fallen; that thereby he may repent but little, go to confession late: put off communion, fear to minister: turn himself to outer things, dread the cell: seek to gossip and idle, pretend he is weak: neglect what is necessary, search into the business of others: be careless of things divine, turn over in his mind the things of earth. If a man does not drive out all this betimes: he runs into more serious snares of the devil. Again he seeks to wound and overthrow certain weaklings by anger and impatience: and saddens and disturbs them for a little thing lost or taken away: arouses anger, injects suspicion; perverts good actions, sows false for true, and persuades to render evil for good. O wickedness of the deceitful enemy: how many are thy snares and deceits, in every place and time, wounding secretly and unexpectedly. And who shall know them; and number all? God alone, Who knows all secrets, knows the guiles of the devil: Who teaches that we are to be on our guard against them by the sacred scriptures revealed of the Holy Ghost. What therefore shall a man do grievously tempted, and in many ways vexed by the presence of the enemy; who also is charged and ridiculed before others? Whither shall he fly to escape the snares: and hear or see no evils? When shall the time come: to have peace and rest? I have told you and again I tell you, little and great. Our peace is in much patience; in true humility, in contempt of all earthly solace, in the brave endurance of adversities: in the patient expectation of the joys of Heaven. Call to mind therefore, most dearly beloved, in your tribulation the favours of God and His wonderful works, from the beginning of creation even to the consummation of the world: and you shall find that the loving-kindness of God surpasses the malice of men sparing their crimes: that they may amend their life unto better. And when He scourges the pious with adversities: He also shows His love in His chosen ones. They then that reckon stripes as favours, they have peace now: and them a most joyous recompense shall follow in Heaven. For there is full peace and safety from foes: freedom from vice, health from disease: rest from toil. There riches without anxiety, delights without bitterness, knowledge without error; love without feigning, bliss without sorrow: honour without confusion, praise and glory without ceasing. But alas, these good things are not in the world, where all things are mingled with evil; for rare is perfect virtue: seldom is the conscience pure from every stain. And unless divine grace be at hand and a careful custody of the heart: soon the negligent man falls into his accustomed vices and sins. And whence does this come? Because we are born with sin, and from youth we are prone to the pleasures of the flesh; we give ourselves half-heartedly to virtue, we are withdrawn unwillingly from our own ideas: we are entangled in vanities, we examine the affairs of others; and therefore our senses, even after conversion and confession of sins, are more apt to return to the earthly and visible things familiar to them: than to rise to the desire of things heavenly and invisible. It is a grievous pain to a dissipated man to withdraw his mind from the base goods to which his nature is habituated: it is a great task to raise his soul to the goods above and eternal, hidden from the eyes of men. Alas, alas, what anguish of soul: to toil and strive every day against oneself, for the reward of everlasting life.

But the so great goods and immense merits and boundless rewards still lie hid: which God shall most abundantly render hereafter to them that toil, struggle, grieve, and piously endure: according to His promises in the holy gospel: "Behold," He saith, "your reward is great in Heaven: which shall be given you for the short combat and distress in the world." But who can know and tell all the perils of this life: which may befall a man in the place of temptation under the sun? For to the just and to the wicked: many like things equally occur. Often also adversity saddens more: than the gain of good rejoices. If a man is poor: anxiety urges him to acquire possessions. If he is rich: he has fear of losing. Wo then to him who has, and wo to him who has not: for from both sides threaten risks of sin. The Wise Man therefore prays choosing the middle way: and says: "Give me neither beggary, nor riches: give me only the necessaries of life." More than this, my son, seek not. For Christ's sake fear not poverty, beloved of Christ: for willingly to suffer want is virtuous: and the gaining of the kingdom of Heaven. Sweeter often is the dry bread of the poor man hungry: than the loaded table of the rich man sated. More wholesome to the beggar is the drink of water, under a miserable shelter of wood: than abundance of strong wine in the palace of a king. For satiety of food overloads the rich man more: the drinking of wine does more harm to his head: than poor nourishment injures the stomach of the ailing beggar. But holy poverty is very soon exposed to danger in great riches; sobriety in luscious banquets, humility in lofty honours; chastity in friendship with women, devotion in tumult, compunction in laughter: silence in crowds, purity of heart in news, quiet in labours; mildness in adversity, prudence in offices; tranquillity in occupations, discretion in reproofs, the taste for things divine in vain stories. Behold how virtues are dimmed and undermined: by too great frequency of certain doings with seculars. For spiritual sweetness is speedily lost by outward affairs: and the heat of charity besought of God cools and is extinguished through long gossiping. And unless lightness of mind be curbed by compunction, lukewarmness driven out by prayer: peace recovered by reading: the conscience often cleansed by pure and humble confession: accustomed bad habits return, grow, harden, oppress and afflict. Wherefore it is needful that a religious brother admonish chiefly himself, and receive kindly the admonitions of others; exercise great care against his passions, and bravely war against the assault of vices: for without doubt brave fighting is the way to the everlasting joys, to be bestowed on the victors at the finish. Hence Christ, speaking by blessed John in the Apocalypse, earnestly exhorts His faithful soldier to fight:

and to be on his guard against the wickedness of the devil by prayer and sacred studies. "Be thou faithful unto death," He saith, "and I will give thee the crown of life." And again in the same. "To him that overcometh I will give the hidden manna: and a new name written, which no man knoweth but he that receiveth." Whereof blessed Paul saith: "No man shall be crowned: except he strive lawfully." Two precious gifts Christ promises His warrior so that he fail not in the combat against vice; to wit, the manna of divine consolation in the present: and the Crown of everlasting joy in the kingdom of Heaven. Be not therefore, brethren, seduced with empty words by friends in the world, nor heed temporal honours: but hold to the good and right path leading by the regular life to life eternal. Which may our Lord Jesus Christ grant us all after the labours and sorrows of this mortal life: Who for our salvation mightily toiled in the world, fought, grieved, wept, prayed: suffered and being crucified triumphed. Amen.

SERMON XVI

OF THE STRICT JUDGEMENT OF GOD, WHERE ALL CREATURES SHALL ACCUSE US

BE you humbled under the mighty hand of God: that He may exalt you in the time of visitation. Beloved brethren, gravely heed these sacred words of blessed Peter the apostle: which have just been read in his epistle. For he exhorts all to true humility of heart; that a man consider the most sublime power of God over him: and the manifold misery of his own weakness. These two joined together make a man deem humbly of himself: and take pride of no good work. Hence again he saith: "God resisteth the proud: but to the humble He giveth grace." Examine then your hearts open in all things to God: think over the evils of the past, the dangers of the present, the judgements of God to come: and how severely all our works are to be searched. We know not, brethren, how God will judge us. But I fear that our accusers will urge many serious charges against us: of which we now think little. But who are these our accusers? Truly very many: of whom now some are to be mentioned.

The holy angels will accuse us; because we did not obey the divine inspirations: but often rather indulged flesh and blood beyond need.

The terrible and malignant demons will accuse us: alleging the places, times and persons, in which and with whom we have sinned: and have not done due penance.

The holy patriarchs and prophets will accuse us: because we have not followed their good example and faith by our works: who foretold us many good things by the sacred writings concerning Christ and the life to come.

The holy apostles and evangelists will accuse us; because we have so carelessly and lukewarmly trodden that way of perfection, which they learnt from Christ and observed: even after we have entered the cloister, and promised to serve God.

The holy martyrs slain for Christ will accuse us; because we have but feebly imitated their patience, when vexed even in few things: and having fallen to softness of the flesh, scarcely retain a spark of our first fervour.

The holy confessors and all the religious Orders will accuse us: because we have not followed according to our powers their abstinence and labour in watchings and many fasts, in prayers, readings, and holy meditations, as we read of them.

Good pastors, priests and doctors will accuse us: who toiled much for the salvation of souls, for the conversion of sinners, for the discipline of religious, for the consolation of the afflicted: because we have not in the cloister perfectly followed their prudence and their preaching by contempt of the world: nor with sufficient reverence and love gratefully received their books most sweet beyond honey and the honeycomb: nor studiously read, nor diligently given heed to their holy discourses.

The readers, the cantors, the writers and all the books which we have in the choir, in the dormitory, in the refectory, and in our cells for study will accuse us; because we have made little profit of them: but have more often listened to foreign and vain discourses. Therefore they would say, if they could speak: "We have piped to you and you have not danced for the greatness of the joys and the rewards to come which are contained written in our volumes: which God has handed down to you for your comfort and instruction." And again lamenting with the weeping children they would say: "We have mourned for you, and you have not wept for the exceeding miseries and pains to come: which we have frequently denounced to you."

The holy hermits, lovers of the solitary life, separated in mind and body from the world, will accuse us; because we have neglected perfectly to copy their angelic manner of life, and heavenly contemplation in continual prayers and devout meditations, in silence and toils: in renunciation of earthly things and mortification of vices. And so they will rejoice in great glory before God and the angels: but we shall stand ashamed because of the luxuries which we have willingly received.

The holy virgins, saintly widows, and all youths and maidens, observing, with constancy, chastity beloved of God, will accuse us: who although they were frail by sex and age: nevertheless could not be torn away by cruel torments from love and fidelity to their heavenly Spouse. But we with difficulty refrain from the dangers and occasions of sins of the flesh; for the most part fast unwillingly and observe strictness of silence with laxity: foolishly dread the cloister and the retirement of the cell established for peace of heart and preservation of devotion; and alas, often give offence whispering with light words at the instigation of the devil: who is the author of the disturbance of whispering and levity. For many sacred virgins and noble matrons, amid friends and kinsfolk in the world, amid wealth and honours, refrained from pleasures; amid persecutors and mockers, held bravely their purpose of chastity: bore most patiently imprisonment and dungeons, chains, blows, and exile. What then shall we say to this, who are men? For too often we seek to wander abroad: whence we bring back little fruit. Let us blush, dear brethren, that we read of so many glorious saints and holy virgins, old men and maidens suffering: and still we are little able to suffer. Let us follow them doing penance for our sins: whom we cannot follow dying for virtue. Let us all say groaning and weeping: "Have mercy on us, O Lord, spare our sins; grant pardon for all our offences: be appeased by the merits and prayers of Thy saints most gratefully accepted by Thee."

There are moreover many other accusers for us also: to wit, a convenient place, a holy Order, and the religious habit. For even if we have left the world to outward appearance, and wear a religious habit with others: nevertheless we do not so strictly keep the statutes of the Order as we have promised.

Our superiors and directors will accuse us: when they are carefully questioned on each point concerning our good conduct in the presence of Christ. For it is necessary that they say simply the truth of the matter: before Christ the judge Who knows all secrets. Among many things it will be chiefly demanded of them and required of us: whether we have been obedient in all with due reverence; whether we have kept peace and concord with the brethren, saving the discipline of the Order: whether we have celebrated the Divine Office day and night devoutly and attentively, cheerfully and watchfully: whether we have prayed fervently and frequently for benefactors living and dead: whether we have done meet penance for our excesses and shortcomings; whether from charity and loving compassion we have poured out prayers for friends and foes in affliction: whether we have set the common good and obedience before private study and devotion.

Our brothers also will accuse us, seeing our manner of life from morning until evening: because we have not given them good example, watching, praying, toiling, and instant in other devout exercises; but have often spent the precious time of penance fruitlessly: seeking our own ease, and neglecting things profitable.

Men of the world will accuse us, wayfarers and chance guests: because they have seen us wandering outside, light of manners, dissolute of words: well clothed, eating daintily, working little, talking long: late to choir, hastening to the cell and repose. For we are bound to give them and all men an example of holy conduct: because we are made a spectacle to God and angels: and to all who behold us, learned and unlearned, it behoves us to show the way of eternal life: and to bear the repute of a good name.

Moreover the elements will accuse us, and all creatures of Heaven and earth, because of the many services rendered for our use; because we have not shown meet worship to our Creator: and have not paid, as was due and befitting, thanksgiving for blessings bestowed with all the affection of our heart, according to the strength which we have received from God. For since we are in health, and receive without great anxiety from our providers daily necessaries; and willingly accept gratuitous gifts: therefore we are now the more obliged towards God, as guests of the King of Heaven.

The fire will speak: and cry out against our sloth and ingratitude. "I by the order of God my Creator succour you in many ways; I as a faithful servant serve gratis the whole and the sick in the kitchen, in the bakery, in the brewery, in the lavatory and in the church: and as often as necessary I show myself kind to all who wish to warm themselves at the fire. I by the power given me burn straw, turf, stones and wood: I dry the damp, warm the cold, soften the hard, harden the soft: I work in different materials contrary effects, by the wondrous power of God impressed on the laws of nature: that you may have your conveniences: to serve God with joy and great gratitude. For in winter I warm your hands and feet; I light the candles, put darkness to flight: render to your eyes the brightness of light. What should I do that I have not done? Answer thy Creator: if I have refused to obey His command. For I have done without contradiction both for the good and the bad: whatever the Lord my Creator, the almighty and merciful God, commanded to be done. For the good indeed and the just I give heat and light to their profit: but for the bad and ungrateful I flame unto vengeance. And when God in anger bids, then I burn cities, towns and castles: and waste both the rich and the poor without respect of persons; and reduce to ashes all the joy, beauty and abundance of the world; and still remain unharmed in the form of my own nature."

The air will say: "I provide a good breeze and serenity that you may walk with ease: toil with ingenuity, sow with fruit: and gather the ripened harvest into the barns and stores of men. But because men often abuse good gifts to work vanities and unlawful gains: God, angered by their malice, of a sudden compels me to work terrors on land, on sea, on trees, on beasts, on castles, on towns, on fields, and on holy houses. For while it is still bright day and nobody is heeding, I raise clouds, produce winds, send forth lightnings, beget thunders, arouse storms, disturb the sea, cast down hail, pour out rain, strike the earth, tear up trees, overthrow houses, and show with terror the power of God over these lower creatures; that all the sinners of the earth may learn to fear God: and weigh from present evils, how dreadful shall be the judgement to come on the last day."

The water will say. "I water the earth with showers, produce springs and rivers, nourish fishes of divers kinds, strongly carry ships and galleons laden with much wealth, and with the blowing of the wind bear them to distant lands and islands: I show many wonderful works of God to them that travel on the sea and in many waters; that they may proclaim His works with exultation when they arrive in port: and give thanks generously as delivered from great dangers. And because sins exact penalty, therefore when God is grievously offended I often strike and destroy ships with a tempest: often I drown men, drink in precious wealth, and cast to the bottom as the mud of the streets the gold and silver wherein men trust; so that thereby the avaricious and proud mighty ones, who oppress the poor and defraud the innocent, may not boast in their riches, nor place their hope in earthly things: but in the living God Who made all things out of nothing, and feeds the poor in little. I wash the hands and feet of the saints, and I serve in many ways the evil and ungrateful; I give drink to the thirsty, fill wells and canals, cleanse stains, make garments white: and from springs and torrents I produce sweet waters for various uses of men and beast. I because of the sins of men was changed into blood in the land of Egypt: against nature I flowed most plentifully from the rock in the desert; at the prayers of the saints I was changed into sweetness: and at the word of Christ into the taste of the best wine. They then are obliged to render many thanks to God who have abundance of water, and take fishes with their nets: but those who inebriate themselves with wine and various liquors and to the poor give little or nothing: shall be tormented with the rich man in Hell."

The earth will say: "I support men and brutes; I offer smooth ways and straight paths to wayfarers through fields and woods: I employ as a rampart mountains and hills lest the waters prevail. I nourish trees, grasses and various kinds of herbs: I bring forth vines and olives, figs and pomegranates, apples, pears, nuts, almonds, beans, peas, barley, wheat, flowers, roses, lilies, violets: and every year I render the usual return to the cultivators of the earth and the harvesters. And for all these blessings freely bestowed upon men, naught else do I ask and hold as thanks: but that everywhere all the nations of the earth, and the islands of the peoples know, serve, preach, praise and worship God; and above all goods visible and invisible love, honour and exalt Him: as long as they live, smell, breathe, tread the earth, dig, plant and build. I also after the death of the flesh receive the bodies of the dead into my lap as a mother her children deprived of light: for of the earth all were made, and unto the earth all shall return as to their mother, whence Adam was formed: and as to the common hospice of all mortal pilgrims. For when any man becomes useless to the world, either worn out with old age, or slain in battle, or infected by disease, or repulsive in appearance, and nobody will now retain him in the house, or nurse him in bed; then without long delay friends and neighbours have recourse to me, make ready a pit, and bring their castaway to me: and beneath my shelter hide him in the ground. And him whom they had loved in life, and praised and honoured highly: now dead they avoid, close their nostrils, dread to gaze on him, and depart. But I, the earth created by God, full of compassion, abhor and spurn no dead man however miserable a Lazarus, or wounded, or fetid; but without respect of persons I receive universally all the sons and daughters of Adam: who because of the sin of their first parent are compelled to return to the dust, whence all took their origin. I open indifferently to poor and rich a place of burial; and if sometimes the living quarrel for a more worthy position: the dead however are silent, and contradict not them that bury them. All the kings of the earth, all princes, all dukes, counts, barons, military leaders, nobles, commoners, prelates, abbots, doctors, lawyers, priests, clerics and laics, in a small hut I enclose, cover and keep: until at the sound of the last trumpet Christ shall appear in His majesty with the holy angels in the greatest glory. For then I am compelled to give up again the bodies sleeping in their graves: to present in judgement without delay all the good and bad with their bodies: that each may receive reward or punishment according to his works which he did in life. Nor then shall I be able to keep back by violence anyone, nor by prayer nor bribe hide longer from the face of the Judge and from the wrath of the Lamb, nor protect by arms: for the just Lord shall judge justly all the bounds of the earth: saving the righteous in mercy: and most justly condemning the wicked for their demerits." O would that all mortals would weigh these things: and frequently think with fear and groaning of the severe judgement of God. For, as the apostle says, we shall all stand before the judgement seat of Christ, to render an account of every past evil action: all creatures accusing us, as has been said, the angels standing round and the demons hungrily waiting to take with them the damned into the fire. There no man shall be able to excuse himself nor appeal to his excellence the Emperor: nor with apostolic letters or royal privileges defend himself against the sentence of the Judge beholding all things from eternity; Who knows with clear knowledge the most hidden thoughts and works of each accomplished in whatsoever age and hour: and that without any report being made to Him. Whose awful judgement we should all fear now: and before the day of judgement and the hour of death repent with true sorrow of heart of all our evils, and humbly crave for pardon: lest haply snatched on a sudden from this world to the judgement, we be for ever condemned with the wicked. May the merciful God grant us, now and ever to find mercy before the throne of His grace: that we may merit to be blessed with the elect: and happily brought into the kingdom of glory. Amen.

SERMON XVII

OF SHUNNING VAINGLORY AND PURSUING HUMBLE OBEDIENCE

HE that glorieth: let him glory in the Lord. Beloved brethren, if you think over your past life in the world with sorrow of heart, and how much you have offended God: in what can you glory? If also you will ponder attentively your daily negligences and divers offences; whence have you cause to glory, who are so imperfect? He who watchfully heeds his past sins, and present dangers, and strictly weighs them: can never vainly glory of his works. Which of us knows how God regards and judges our every thought, word, and deed day and night; whether He accepts, or rejects them? A man also, however good and devout he may be now, knows not how long he will remain thus: whether he will become better or worse. Brethren, if you begin to think of the hidden judgements of God, His terrible works upon the sons of men from the commencement of the world: very soon will fade away everything lofty and carnal that gives pleasure in earthly things. Whence holy David prays: "Pierce Thou my flesh with Thy fear: for I am afraid of Thy judgements." As God is loving and merciful towards the penitent and them that fervently amend: so is He harsh and terrible to them that do ill and negligently. Do not therefore glory in the malice and wickedness of your heart: as many fools do; who stained with filth are not ashamed: but even when mocked by others rejoice and laugh. Lift your eyes to Heaven, and look upon the dignity, purity and supreme blessedness of the angels: who seek not their own praise nor the glory of another, but the glory, honour, and magnificence of God: by Whom they acknowledge that they were created, in Whom also they love one another: and most gratefully ascribe to Him all that they have received from Him with mighty power. If therefore the holy angels are humble and grateful to God in such sublime heights: how much more man, mortal and a sinner, ought to humble himself, and cast away all vainglory. Learn, wretched and proud man, not to be high-minded, but with heart and mouth consent to the humble; that thou mayest find grace before God and the angels: which the puffed-up cannot attain, and that thou mayest not lose everlasting glory in Heaven, which the bad angels forfeited by pride. Strive to wish to please God alone in every good work: and to submit thyself to every human creature for God's sake; to obey the seniors, assist the juniors, show reverence to all: bear with gentleness the conduct of the sick and the perverse. If thou seekest to be saved, if thou wilt be made happy and exalted: follow the humble Christ, and despise thyself. For thou canst not otherwise mount up to Heaven: unless thou humble thyself with thy whole heart for God's sake. Desire not to be in the mouth of men: who with foolish praises deceive the silly lover of temporal glory. See into thy heart in truth, to how many passions it is exposed; and thou shalt not glory in thyself: nor despise thy neighbour, however poor he be and weak. Hold in mind the memorable word of Christ; and when the vainglory of the world tempts thee: answer thyself what Christ said to the Jews. "If I glorify myself: My glory is nothing." Let vainglory then depart and the praise of men for any learning or art acquired: let foolish boasting of good work or skilful discourse cease: let worldly cunning be uprooted from the heart of a religious: perish false imagining of holiness shown without: let the presumption of novelty blush, void of the fruit of charity, contrary to the peace of the community. Rejoice ever, simplicity of the dove, free from the gall of bitterness; correct thy brother in the spirit of mildness: teach rather by humble example than by subtle word. Bear with patience the adversary: whom thou canst not amend to perfection. The time will soon come, that iniquity shall stop her mouth: and the wickedness of the deceiver shall fall on his own head; and he will bear his own shame, who eagerly desires human praise: and seeks the dignity of honour. What holiness does the report of a great name bring: when little or no virtue dwells in the conscience? What devotion does wandering through divers countries bestow: which is the cause of great vanity, and a distraction of the mind? What profit does acquaintance with the mighty afford a religious; and the curious gazing at high walls and castles? In sooth all these things are made of the earth: and unto the earth all shall return. Often also by the power of arms they are brought down to dust: and burnt with fire. Better therefore is a poor man living unknown in a wretched hut eating herbs and vegetables with a good conscience; than a rich man dwelling in a fine mansion, drinking wines and eating delicacies with mirth and pride: filled with an evil conscience. To whom may be justly applied that word of the gospel: "Thou fool, this night do they require thy soul of thee: and whose shall those things be which thou hast provided?" Let no one then be glad for the vain praises of men: even if he do aught praiseworthy. Let no man trust too much in his own goodness: or foolishly presume of his own strength: or also boast of nobility of race. Let no man be puffed up for possession of knowledge; let no man boast of the dignity of superior-ship over others: let no man, trusting in abundance of wealth and revenue, think himself happy and rich, nor despise the poor; for he knows not how long he will live and possess these things: he knows not what trouble may thence come to him, when God shall so permit. In fine, in every temporal thing and human work: uncertain is the progress and good issue. For very often things fall out otherwise than men think: and often counsels are changed to the contrary. Blind men cannot see mountains on a clear day: however clever they may be. The wise in their own eyes are often mistaken concerning the future: who, trusting in their own cunning, have not God before their eyes. For those who ambition earthly things, love honours, pursue pleasures, fear misfortunes, desire prosperity, seek high places, rejoice in vanities; by a just judgement of God will mourn in their turn: and will be miserably afflicted for good things lost. Betwixt the hope of good and the fear of evil the worldly and fleshly heart is constantly tossed; because it has not set the anchor of its hope in the desire of Heaven: where all good things abound and last for ever. Wherefore, most dear brethren, since no one knows for certain what of things to come may be more advantageous for him, or more expedient for the salvation of his soul: it is safer and more praiseworthy to follow the counsel of the wise and experienced, and especially of our prelates and ancients: who have the knowledge of the scriptures, and experience of dangers from themselves and many others. For often the devil with malicious instinct: beguiles the devout even under the appearance of good. Let no one therefore be headstrong in his own desire and private fancy: nor rashly abound in his own opinion and natural gifts: but even in small things not sufficiently well known to him let him proceed with caution: seek advice, act with deliberation, tell his motive: expose the secret wound of his mind, trust the physician: deceive not himself under feigned words: nor speak otherwise with the mouth than he holds in the heart: because it is written, "Thou wilt destroy all that speak a lie." It is a ruling of law, he who speaks falsely gains nothing: but renders himself unworthy of all favour, and makes himself suspect to very many. It is a great and praiseworthy prudence: to renounce one's own industry, humbly to obey the superior; to believe one more learned, to agree with one more experienced: and ever to show oneself cheerful in all good things pleasing to God. Nor is danger of error to be feared there: where the good intention of the prelate excuses the obedient disciple. Finally all religious bound to Christ may be safely advised: that all the matter of their perplexity, all desire of devotion, all study of reading, all leisure of contemplation, all the fruit of their preaching, and whatever good they may conceive in their mind: they first take care to offer to God in secret prayer; then this same humbly expose in open confession to their superior, as to the vicar of Christ: and unhesitatingly commit to them what they ought to do or leave undone. For perfect obedience ought to have nothing of its own seeking: possess neither great nor little with disordered affection: that thereby all cupidity and self-ease having been uprooted as much as possible: the soul may have a free flight to Heaven. To such a one to live is now Christ: and to die daily for Christ the greatest gain. And to be with Christ the only desire: and most blissful good. Brethren, ever hold firmly in your heart the word of the wise Solomon: who sets simple obedience with resignation of self-will before all sacrifices, saying: "Obedience is better than victims." And again: "Do all things with counsel: and thou shalt not repent when thou hast done."

AN EXAMPLE

There were two Devout Brothers in the Deventer Congregation engaged in study: and they were speaking together of the virtue of obedience. Said one therefore to the other, his fellow: "It has always gone ill with me: when neglecting advice I have done my own will." Answered the other. "And I have never regretted: that I have yielded to good counsels." I know an old Brother who in his youth very willingly listened to the words of the elders; but he grieves greatly of this: that he has left much to forgetfulness.

SERMON XVIII

OF THE SPIRITUAL WARFARE AGAINST VICES

WHEN you shall hear of wars and seditions: be not terrified. Beloved brethren, in this life we are in the midst of enemies: and from all sides the war to be waged against vices presses on us. Daily we are tempted and attacked: now indeed softly, at another time bitterly, but always perilously and wickedly: the devil everywhere laying snares and harassing us. For no man living is wholly free from temptations and disturbances as long as the spirit bides in the body: but everyone is forced even against his will to bear the burden of the day and the heats. Let no one therefore grow slothful in idleness; let no one think of departing from the camp of God: let no one lay down his arms before the end of the war. Let the new soldier be girded with a new sword to combat in fervour of spirit against the wickedness of the devil; let him fight bravely with the two-edged sword: having together the fear and the love of God in his mind: seeking the retirement of prayer: shunning above all publicity and sloth. For no man shall be crowned in Heaven: unless he has lawfully striven against his passions and vices in this world. The new sword is the fresh fervour of holy devotion; which at the beginning of conversion is often given by a loving illumination of the Holy Ghost to new soldiers: to enable them to battle bravely against the temptations to come. Let the novice then take diligent heed that he lose not the grace of devotion by being infected with sloth; but at all times let him make himself ready for the spiritual combat: and often pray: that he may be one of the chosen servants of Abraham, who overcame his foes armed by faith and prayer. Let him often sharpen his sword renewing his first purpose which he undertook; now meditating on the Passion of the Lord: now on the combats and bloody wounds of the martyrs: now on the flames of the eternal fire, now on the great horror of the demons: now on the unbearable stench of the pitch and sulphur, now on the lamentable crying of the damned: now on the despair of all salvation. These things, if they come to the mind, shake off sloth: repress the concupiscence of the flesh; consume the rust of vices, reprove negligence: and mightily enkindle to spiritual progress, and the fervour of devotion. Let every lukewarm religious then fear exceedingly: let the wanderer and the dissipated restrain himself: lest he come to that place of torments, where there is no issue, nor room for mercy. But now in the time of grace, let him strive to amend his past negligences: let him cleanse the secret of his heart by humble confession and devout prayer: let him recollect himself by holy reading and frequent compunction of heart: let him curb lightness of words, by the keeping of silence; let him bring back the tranquillity of internal peace, by the forgetfulness of exterior affairs: let him drive out the inrushing filth of evil thoughts, by the pure meditation of heavenly things; and to appease the anger of God more speedily: let him hold to true humility. These things appertain to manly and warlike beginners; who because of the three battalions of the enemy are bidden to stand to arms: and strenuously combat all their life against the flesh, the world and the devil.

It behoves then to fight with the help of God by being instant in prayer: by refraining from delicacies, patiently bearing adversities, as did all the saints, and especially the martyrs of Christ: who striving most bravely overcame their foes by gently enduring: and after many insults and torments, guiltlessly dying. They heeded not friends and relatives according to the flesh: nor temporal riches and honours; but the meriting of eternal rewards, heavenly treasures, triumphal crowns: and unfading glory. For by transitory torments: they deserved to pass without delay to everlasting joys. Now their souls rejoice in Heaven: who followed Christ's footsteps in reproaches and most grievous pains.

The holy confessors also strove, living soberly, justly and piously: often fasting, watching, praying, meditating, studying: groaning, weeping, supplicating for their own and others' sins: bearing contumely, detractions, mockery, murmuring, threats, exactions, losses and wrongs: persevering in a right faith, firm hope and perfect charity even unto death.

The holy and grave doctors of holy Church strove also, disputing against heretics and divers errors, zealously preaching the word of God; writing, studying, dictating books: raising questions, solving doubts, throwing light on the obscure; rebuking vices, proposing a saving doctrine, urging men to the godly and profitable; warning the simple from curious, intricate and fruitless side-issues: arousing the slothful, reproving the hardened: consoling the sad, strengthening the weak: and daily showing others a good example of life: so that what they could not persuade by words: they affirmed by holy actions.

The holy hermits and monks, and the professed of divers Orders also strove, renouncing the world: spurning the vanities of the world and the delights of the flesh, treading under foot temporal glory and honour: fleeing the tumult of men, loving solitude: forsaking their own, taking up their cross: chastising their body by abstinence, curbing the tongue by silence: shunning wanderings and discourses, doing themselves violence day after day: freely submitting themselves to the yoke of holy obedience, strictly living in the cloister under the regular discipline: imitating the apostolic perfection and for Christ's sake giving themselves to daily crucifixion: combatting with a perfect heart all inordinate affections and their own motions: keeping back nothing to themselves of all things dear, utensils, books or clothing. There is nothing in sooth more perfect, more wholesome, more profitable, more praiseworthy, more secure and more restful unto having a good conscience and peace of heart: than that the religious, devout to God and a professed monk, should every hour without contradiction, without delay, without dislike, readily and willingly obey his superior: bravely overcoming himself, humbly submitting, patiently bearing things burdensome and bitter. To keep this way of perfection is required a great struggle, against the inclination of sensuality, against the prudence of one's own opinion, against one's evil habit and the licence of the flesh, which will be subjected, ruled and restrained by others unwillingly: but seeks rather to wander, to enjoy and to amuse itself. For these things are very contrary to the law God and reason and the common peace of the brethren: and the good government of the cloister. Wherefore the simple obedient brother will be reckoned very praise-worthy and truly lovable: who with cheerful countenance and willing heart is ready to serve all after the example of Jesus Christ: keeping the law of life and discipline for the salvation of his soul in the Order of Regulars. Again very culpable and blameworthy is the cunning brother, abounding in his own sense; who does not humbly obey his superior: showing him reverence and submission. Wo to him who unwillingly or with feigned heart obeys: and murmurs from slight cause. This one Christ, obeying His Father, sternly rebukes, and often is wont severely to punish in the present life. For He says to the rulers of the church: "He that heareth you, heareth Me: and he that despiseth you, despiseth Me." What therefore he said to the apostles, this He says likewise to their successors and to other prelates: this He addresses to superiors of monasteries also: bidding subjects obey them for God's sake, for the sake of great merit, and good example: for He will give grace and glory to all who are obedient: but to the disobedient and perverse confusion and punishment everlasting.

For the man truly obedient and submissive to the higher powers ordained by God: is compared to a wise merchant; who in every place and money market thinks of increasing his gain, and guarding against losses: endeavours to buy of good value, and not to be ensnared with worthless articles. So also the religious bound by the chain of obedience ought to think and strive in every work and business committed to him; to act faithfully, overlooking naught that pleases God: and that the superior entrusts to him. For then especially he makes progress in good, and enlarges his merit: if spurning the visible things of the world, he aims at the heavenly: if he deems it gain to his soul beyond all wealth to be submissive to the beck of another. For the fruit of obedience is better: than the thought carefully worked out of one's own prudence. And much more fruitful is the will forsaken for God's sake: than long study and perfect psaltery. Blessed therefore the religious of whatsoever Order and state: who follows Christ now by the cross and violence to the flesh always ready to obey: because in the end at his death he shall receive with the holy confessors a special reward in Heaven: as Christ promises and says in these words: "Well done, thou good and faithful servant, because thou hast been faithful over a few things: enter into the joy of thy Lord." Let not then a man base and ignorant, dust and ashes to be, disdain to subject himself and obey a man who gives wholesome advice; when an angel obeys an angel indicating anything to him by a mere sign, and holy Gabriel sent by God immediately comes to announce to Mary the incarnation of Christ. But this is more to be admired, and is set before us all as an example; that God obeyed man, served, and humbly bowed Himself to things lowly and base: that it might not be burdensome to anyone, however great, learned, or noble, to obey a greater, or even an equal or a lesser: since Christ did all this before him. For He obeyed Joseph and His Mother, leaving the Temple and the doctors, where He could have favour and honour: and He went down with His parents to Nazareth, and was subject to them: where He remained long unknown to many friends how great He was.

The holy virgins also and the continent widows bravely strove against their foes: who in the love of Jesus Christ overcame the vanities of the world and the pleasures of the flesh and the temptations of the devil in a tender age and weak sex: continuing in prayers, watchings and fasts, shunning worldly company and useless discourses, chastising their bodies, refraining from all superfluous adornment: desiring to please God alone with sincere mind and chaste body, daily preparing themselves by holy desires and interior sighs, for the heavenly nuptials; beautifying as with white flowers the bridal chamber of the heart by devout meditations, hymns, psalms, washing away the stains of the conscience with contrition and confession: and panting unceasingly with sighing and burning love for the presence of the heavenly and invisible Spouse. O sacred trophy of virgins; brave bands of maidens, widows and noble matrons: who for the sake of the love of the heavenly Spouse, and to preserve the beauty of angelic purity, despised earthly nuptials, the love of men, the patrimony of parents, the comfort of children, the banquets of acquaintance; the ornaments of dress, the splendour of gems, abundance of plate, gold rings, silver goblets, divers furniture, silk tapestry, painted chairs, the ministry of servants, the attendance of maids, the music of instruments; the sight of games, and all the pleasures of worldly joys: which this vain and frivolous world presents and flaunts before the eyes of the unwise. For these things have profited and do profit nothing to their lovers: who rejoice in perishable and foolish things, full of deceits and sorrows.

Happy therefore the band of holy virgins; who strove for eternal life to reject as dung all the joys of this world and bodily adornments: and desired rather to be made happy with the angels and archangels in heavenly glory. O truly happy assembly of maidens, who abided constant in their station: and even to the shedding of blood resisted vices and the laws of tyrants. Therefore most beautiful crowns in Heaven adorned with precious gems and jewels: have they merited to receive with glorious praise from Christ for the victory of their combat. For who can ever worthily and fully unfold, what distresses they often endured in their heart: what temptations in the flesh: what suggestions from the demons they felt in prayer: who urged them to the pleasures of the world away from the chastity of Christ. Alas, what counsels Satan devised by the persuasions of friends: by the flattery of matrons, by manifold mockery also and terrors: to seduce them and draw them with him through fleeting delights to infernal pains. But by the pity and help of Christ their Maker, the wiles of the devil prevailed naught against the maiden battalions; nor the clamour of wicked men, nor the blows of tyrants: nor the weapons threatening death. Because the love of Christ stronger than all armour, nobler than all honour, lovelier than all beauty, sweeter than all melody: so mightily burned in the virgin hearts and female hosts armed with the sign of the cross; that they feared to suffer neither flames nor blows, nor beasts, nor prisons, nor hunger, nor death: in order to preserve an unshaken faith and the gem of chastity in a pure heart and body to be crowned with perpetual honour in Heaven. These combats then of the blessed martys, and long and hard abstinence of the holy confessors, and especially the chastity, patience and perseverance of the sacred virgins you ought to place before you to be imitated: and to arm yourselves manfully to resist vices and passions. I exhort all in charity: that for a shield in the combat you neglect not the intercession of the saints; that you faint not in your temptations: by the gift of Our Lord Jesus Christ the Rewarder of all the good. Amen.

SERMON XIX

OF THE DIVERS WARS AND PERILS OF THIS LIFE

THE flesh lusteth against the spirit, and the spirit against the flesh: for these are contrary one to another. Beloved brethren, in the preceding sermon you heard a little about the spiritual warfare of the saints: now consequently a few words must be said of the different kinds of war, in order to guard against the snares and wiles of the old serpent; who full of malice goes about like a roaring lion seeking whom he may devour: and cruelly rages in particular against young soldiers of Christ. For he envies them the glory of the heavenly kingdom: whence he fell with many on a sudden by pride. By whose pestiferous persuasion very many are deceived: and sometimes men famous in science and raised high in government have gone astray infected by vainglory: who drawn away by the friendship of men fell and were mortally wounded. But, brethren newly converted, be on your guard against two evils especially: to wit, carnal desires suddenly rushing in through the five senses of the body; and pride of mind by the desire of vain praise: lest you lose the grace of interior devotion with the reward of the eternal recompense. Our fighting, most dear brethren, is not carnal power: but the gentle suffering of all wrongs for Christ: not worldly wisdom: but humble obedience: not the seeking of bodily ease: but affliction of the flesh: not rest from toil: but the mortification of evil pleasure. If you ask how long will last these wars between the flesh and the spirit, between the devil and man, between the world and Christ: I say, according to the gospel and the apostle: until the last span of our life and the consummation of the world. For Christ said before the hour of His Passion: "My soul is sorrowful even unto death." And to His disciples at the Last Supper: "In the world you shall have distress. If they have persecuted Me: they will also persecute you." And therefore encouraging them to patience and perseverance: He said to His friends grieved at His departure: "Let not your heart be troubled nor let it be afraid; for I go to prepare a place for you: that where I am you also may be with Me. But meanwhile while you are in the world: hold to patience as a strong buckler: and to the breast-plate of faith in every danger, trusting always in God." Let us pray then, brothers, that we may find grace and mercy in the sight of Our Lord Jesus Christ: and that He may teach us the art of fighting against our passions and vices: which assault and tempt us as long as we live in the flesh and nourish the body. Let each one say with David in the psalm when he is tempted by any vice at the instigation of the devil: or troubled by a perverse man. "Lord, overthrow them that fight against me lest I fall beneath the burden: for without Thee I cannot resist or endure." For he who is often tempted and in his temptation speedily flies to Christ and prays: will be delivered by His grace, will be strengthened and will prevail: he will progress greatly in the virtue of patience: and will receive a greater crown for his brave struggle. But he who is seldom or never tempted, nor troubled by his own or others' malice: this one is to be called an angel rather than a man. His dwelling is more truly to be sought in Heaven than on earth. For there is supreme peace and concord: but here peace is seldom, joy brief: repose little, distress frequent: anxiety heavy, and victory uncertain. Nevertheless we must not lose heart: because for the least toil and sorrow will be given rejoicing without end.

But the multitude of our wars and the wiles of our foes, who can unfold? No one unless he be enlightened by God: and well learned in Holy Writ, as Paul who saith: "For we are not ignorant of his devices." However, hear a little concerning the wars between the good and the bad from the sacred books for your warning and instruction; that you may be more cautious to withstand the perils of the wicked: and stronger to persevere in the paths of the just.

The first war commenced with the angels in Heaven: when Lucifer by pride wished to lift himself on high, and to be made like to the Most High: and to glory as in his own power: and to take delight in himself alone. When this was discovered in the palace of the heavenly King: St. Michael and his angels, angry at the arrogance of the haughty Lucifer, were moved with the zeal of justice: and cast out all the citizens of pride from their bounds. For no angel, however great, should exalt himself above the magnificence of his Creator: nor being made equal himself to his Maker: nor in the beauty of his wisdom rashly glory: nor abuse the sublime gifts freely bestowed upon him by God. Since then Satan by the swelling of pride exalted himself too high vainly glorying, and raising his throne above the rest: by a just judgement of God he fell from the happy fellowship of the holy angels into the abyss of hell and the prison of the damned. Of whom the Saviour said to His disciples: "I saw Satan like lightning falling from Heaven." Of whose terrible lot, and irreparable fall: blessed John the evangelist speaks in the Apocalypse, saying: "And there was a great battle in Heaven, Michael and his angels fought with the dragon: and the dragon was cast into the earth, and his angels were thrown down with him: neither was their place found any more in Heaven." Behold how much the pride of the devil deserved: who has been cast out from the face of the God of Heaven, that he may not see the glory of God. Which doubtless he can never attain: who wishes to glory in himself. Hence also Isaias exclaims manifestly of the loss of the reprobate: "Let the wicked one be destroyed: that he may not see the glory of God." By a most unquestionable instance it is now evident, how very displeasing to God is the exaltation of the proud. Who spared not the angels in their pride: but delivered them to eternal flames to be tormented, having taken away all hope of forgiveness. Alas, how severe a sentence of the supernal judge, to be cast out from the pleasant face of the divine majesty and everlasting bliss: and ever to be burnt by most fierce flames, which cannot be extinguished by waters, nor mitigated by remedies. Wherefore each must fear because of the severe judgement of God on the proud angels damned eternally: but rather with the psalmist confess and pray: "Let not the foot of pride come tome: and let not the hand of the sinner move me." And again: "Shall not my soul be subject to God: for from Him is my salvation."

The second war commenced in Paradise, when the first man had been made: to wit, between the devil and man, between Eve and the serpent. For the devil envying man hitherto innocent, that he could obtain the entrance to Heaven by obedience to the command: approached in the appearance of a serpent, with a crafty question to the woman, whom he knew to be weaker, and more yielding than the man: and with flattering words and cunning arguments seduced her easily believing him: and not heeding the precept of God at such a crisis. But alas, man formed right by God, and set in the most happy place of Paradise: by the transgression of the sacred precept, lost the state of innocence and the dwelling of sovereign peace: for a morsel of one most miserable apple. Therefore gravely offending God, he incurred the sentence of death, and merited much misery of body and soul: as now truly all we children of Eve experience, suffer and grieve: who by the vice of original sin, are stained, corrupted and stricken. In this war man was vanquished, tempted by an apple: who seduced by the devil's malice, and poisoned with the venom of mortal sin was pierced with many wounds: to wit, hunger, thirst, cold, heat, toil, sweat, plague, sickness, and the horror of death. Alas, he also lost Paradise and Heaven, by the fault of disobedience: through the deceit of the serpent and the folly of the woman. Who too credulous was beguiled by the devil's words in five ways in the five senses of the body: namely, through the listening to a lying discourse, through looking at a beautiful colour, through touching the fatal apple, through smelling a nice odour, and through tasting a sweet savour. But what is worse, having tasted the death-dealing food, she further seduced her husband by flattery and by giving him the unlawful fruit: forbidden them both under pain of death. But when this evil thing had been rashly done, God was angry and cast them forth guilty from the Paradise of pleasure: from the most pleasant and most restful spot of the whole world; and thrust them to do penance into the exile of this world as into a prison, to eat the bread of labour and sorrow all the days of their life: with all their children thereafter to be born of their seed. This war between the devil and man will last: as long as the human race walks upon the earth. And until the number of the elect be filled: the evil one ceases not to persecute the good, his adversaries. But nevertheless the loving and merciful Lord God compassionating fallen man: said to the serpent fatuous, envious and malicious: "I will put enmities between thee and the woman: and thy seed and her seed"; designating Christ to be born of a woman: and to redeem the human race. "She," He said, "shall crush thy head: and thou shalt lie in wait for her heel." From these words we see the wickedness and malice of the devil against us: that we are not to believe him, or parley with him, or argue with him: because he is more cunning than all living things upon the earth: and more subtle than all who study in the schools and in the affairs of the world. Beware, novices, of the head of the serpent, the beginning of temptation: the poison of the snake lies hid under the grass: who often comes and deceives a child under the seeming of a beautiful apple rotten within. But he deceives not only the simple and laics but the learned also and famed masters and religious: suggesting to them divers vanities. He tempts almost every day by the five senses of the body: now enticing by the flesh: now lifting up by the spirit: now by making angry with wrath. Or likewise he makes men to quarrel for honours and riches: to rejoice in luxuries: or to be too much saddened in adversities and earthly losses. These are the works of the devil: who fell from the height of Heaven by pride. He made the children of Israel murmur for the fatigue and want of food in the desert: he persuaded the Jews to sacrifice to idols in the temple consecrated to God. He tempted Christ three times after a long fast: he sowed cockle among the wheat: a traitor among the apostles; a murmurer among the disciples: among the deacons a seducer, among the faithful a persecutor of the faith. He seduced Judas by theft: from theft he drew him to the noose: from the noose he dragged the miserable man to hell. There there is no redemption: nor any refreshment. Alas, all who consent to him he induces to sin against God and the neighbour: and after many evils he persuades to destroy themselves: to neglect Heaven and to love the world. Who is it that draws the monk to the world: and to the tumults of men? The devil the ensnarer of souls. Who is it that draws the cleric from the choir to the marketplace? The devil the forger of every guile: desirous of hindering the divine worship. Who is it that draws the lay-brother from labour to idleness and gossip? The devil going round the world, to find somebody wandering abroad: and toiling little or nothing for the community. Who holds down the slothful in bed: that called he may not immediately arise? The devil closing the eyes of the sleepy, that he may yet lie a little, and satisfy his drowsiness. For he rejoices over the lazy one: and him that often comes late. Who sows discords among the brethren: and begets many suspicions in them? The devil the disturber of peace, the inventor of wickedness, the father of lying, the concealer of truth, the author of guile, the encourager of partiality. Who teaches to love pleasures, to shun labours, to desire honours: to eat and drink well, to dress grandly? The devil the inciter of gluttony, the mover of wrath, the thief of chastity, the ensnarer of clerics, the tempter of monks, the harasser of virgins, the assaulter of the continent, the seducer of the innocent, the mocker of the simple, the overthrower of the wise, the detractor of the good, the praiser of the wicked, the hinderer of devotion, the procurator of dissipation. Let it not displease you to have noted these things of the wars and thousand arts and wiles of the devil: that you observe greater caution and more strict watch against every temptation and suggestion of his whatsoever. Because as it is said by many, and frequently experienced, the devil never ceases from the malice of doing harm: nor does he suffer others to rest: but where he himself does not come: he sends his fellows to vex the little sheep of Christ. And if he cannot carry off and is forbidden to slay: at least he strives to injure them by terrors. And if he sees one wandering, and idling from good work or study or prayer; he approaches the more freely to tempt him: because he has incautiously laid down the arms that resist the foe.

A third war is called the intestine struggle, which has arisen between the flesh and the spirit; the flesh lusting against the spirit from the penalty of sin: and the spirit struggling by reason against sensuality. This rebellion the first man had not felt in the state of innocence: because the spirit subject to God peacefully ruled the powers of the body by the curb of reason. But this intestine war is most cruel and most troublesome to us all begotten and born in corruptible and sinful flesh. For what is more cruel and troublesome to every man desiring peace: than daily to fight against himself, to struggle against nature, to restrain lust, to overcome concupiscence pricking within? O servant of God, O soldier of Christ: hear a counsel good and profitable to thee. Guard thy sight: close thy hearing: touch not the unlawful: flee the harmful. And if thou feelest the goad: give not consent. Nothing so toilsome as to begin anew;

from morning unto evening to stand against the three battalions: to cast the darts of prayer at the enemy; to sound the sacred trumpets, to groan in the heart, to cry with the voice: frequently to doubt of the victory of triumph. Whence unless the Lord be nigh to us: our weakness shall never be able to resist such perils. An exceedingly heavy burden and an intricate war, to nurse the flesh, to nourish an enemy, to clothe, warm, wash, dry, caress it that it murmur not, chastise it that it rebel not: encourage it that it lose not hope, rebuke it that it grow not slothful, subdue it that it be not puffed up; strengthen it that it faint not, beat it that it resist not, instruct it that it err not, repress it that it grow not insolent: love its nature as a companion, but hate its lust as the snare of death. Finally, it is not lawful to kill the flesh: no man can rid himself of it; it is not beseeming to obey it, one must not too quickly believe it, it is not expedient to parley with it: it is generally hurtful to smile upon it. What then shall be done? Let the flesh serve the spirit, readily obey, toil, sweat, fast, rise, watch, pray, sing, and praise: until after brief labour it receive everlasting repose. This flesh therefore frail, mortal, full of concupiscence, unmastered, and often rebellious to the spirit, reason ought to rule and fear curb, dignity moderate, discipline restrain, righteousness adorn, modesty defend, sobriety temper, justise chastise when it sins: prudence instruct when it errs, discretion consider that there be naught excessive. The spirit therefore searching all things as an active pilot should carefully keep an eye on the carnal mind and youthful soul, lest it cleave to its own opinion; lest it grow slothful in leisure, or seek softness, or flee austerity: but that it quickly rise to prayer, come betimes to choir; pass readily to labour, shun idle wandering round: strictly keep silence, love the quiet of the cell; often pray, willingly study, willingly write: do each action at its due time, set the common interest before all private concerns: blush not to serve inferiors, hasten to obey superiors, joyously embrace every command; rejoice supremely to assist at the divine praises, prefer to be at leisure to God within: and deem it the better part to be entangled in no exterior affairs. Albeit then it be hard and troublesome to thee to war daily against the incentives of the flesh; nevertheless it is extremely virtuous and meritorious to resist concupiscence, and to do violence to nature: which is most viciously inclined to its own ease and the things that please it. And unless it be speedily withstood by abstention and restraint; it seduces the soul and draws it to consent: as Eve deceived Adam enticing him, and giving him the forbidden fruit to eat. In this warfare no man is overcome, unless corrupted by an evil will, and of his own accord turned away from God. For whosoever follows the desire of the flesh, quickly falls into vice unless be hold to the rein of reason. Beware then of the dangers in the daily conflict of the flesh: for as long as we live in this world eating, drinking, we are tempted in divers ways. Whence also a certain prophet, warns slothful and soft souls to watchfulness of conscience, saying: "From her that sleepeth in thy bosom: keep the doors of thy mouth." That is, firmly restrain without all the senses of thy body; lest death enter by the windows of the body to the interior of the heart: and the devil ensnare thee with his nets.

Brothers, if you do manfully and strive, and call Christ to your aid; you can certainly merit much more in this war of the flesh: than if you felt no burden within you. Have therefore always a good trust in God: and cease not to pray, and to fight against vice. Many in truth and great goods are concealed in this combat: which give pleasure to God in the weak flesh. But you shall receive great rewards with a certain hope of glory to come from the just judge, even for the least grief of heart, and pain of body however slight. All burdens also borne for the love of Christ will rejoice your souls very much at the end of your life: as a certain devout sister being in her agony said: "Up to this it has been suffering, up to this it has been struggle: now comes the reward." What more shall I say to them that fight against their flesh? All things whatsoever that you do by virtue of obedience, or that you endure in the Order for the strictness of discipline and the love of justice, shall be written in the book of life: although sometimes the flesh may complain ftom frailty. But if the devil move you with some indignation, or evil suspicion against a superior giving a command, or a brother not doing well, or speaking ill: do not therefore leave aside the good begun: but rather perfect what you have commenced for the honour of God and the edification of the neighbour. For then the most wicked ensnarer and hinderer of all good, the devil, will speedily fly from you: when he is scorned and not heeded. For all his whisperings of the world, of the flesh, of riches, of earthly glory: are full of poison and deceit. Many in old age now bewail: that in youth they acted so foolishly, and offended God. Stand then and fight for your soul: in religion and in a holy congregation. For whatever ill you suffer in toils and pains, in heat and cold, in watchings and fasts, in abstinence from flesh and white-meats, in want of wine and better drink for the destruction of vice and the acquisition of virtues: all this shall be reckoned unto you for the greatest gains and rewards in the kingdom of Christ above thousands of gold and silver, and all the desirable things of the world. For what more worthy: than to be the friend of God? what more happy than to be numbered among the children of God? What more rich; than to have part in the kingdom of Christ? What more pleasant: than to assist at the rejoicings of the angels? What more noble: than to be crowned in the presence of God and the sight of all the saints? O how delightful and joyous it will be to the soul combating and loving

God, to be borne by the angels into Heaven: and with Lazarus once poor to be made glad in eternal repose, for the brief toil and slight pain suffered in the body; for the coarse clothing and tasteless food, for the hard bed and oft-interrupted sleep: for the tears shed and the devout prayers; for the holy meditations, and many other good exercises and sacred readings: accomplished in obedience and patience. O holy obedience and happy patience for Christ: which opens the gate of Heaven to him who is about to die.

A fourth war is called a domestic duel: which arose between two brothers german, exceedingly cruel and pernicious: by the instigation of the devil and the burning of envy. For as is read in the Book of Genesis, when two sons had been born to Adam, envious Cain rose up against his brother Abel, just and beloved of God: whose offerings are said to have been accepted by God. Whence cruelly moved in a wrath of fury, as a ravenous wolf he raged against the gentle lamb; and resolved to kill his innocent brother, better than himself: not fearing God, nor ashamed to sadden his parents: but excited by a malicious soul he stretched out his evil hands: and the first among men committed murder. From these two brothers quarrelling, many discords and partialities among men have arisen; in divers regions and places, in cities and towns, brawling with one another for primacy and wealth. From this occasion as rivalry everywhere increased, befell also the persecution of the wicked against the life of the just, as the holy histories of the saints show: and the divers chronicles of heathens and Christians contain, which treat fully of the wars of Trojans, Romans, and many kings and divers peoples. As it was from the beginning of the world between the sons of Adam, strife and struggle, jealousy and brawl; and especially between the miserly and the ambitious to have and increase earthly goods: so still in these days men quarrel for perishable things and vain honours. And it is to be feared that after us also these things will continue until the Lord shall come manifestly on the last day to judge all the ends of the earth. For then when Christ appears in His Majesty and glory: it shall be rendered to each man according to his works. Then all the strifes and wars of the wicked shall cease: and all scandals shall be taken away from the kingdom of God. Then shall the mouths of them that speak evil things be silent: and the bones of the saints that were humbled shall rejoice. Then shall be heard from the mouth of the just judge one final and irrevocable sentence: "Go ye cursed into everlasting fire: come ye blessed of My Father, possess ye the kingdom prepared for you from the foundation of the world." But meanwhile as long as one generation passeth away and another generation cometh: all things are mingled together in our earth, full of thorns and briars. Now joyous things come, now sad: now hunger torments, now thirst burns; now fear casts down, now hope lifts up: now toil wearies, now repose refreshes; now health delights, now sickness weakens: and after a short while overhanging death consumes all things beautiful and pleasant. In every place then, and state, and order, the good are found mingled with the bad; the gentle with the froward, the humble with the proud: the peaceful with the passionate, the devout with the dissolute; the bashful with the bold, the silent with the talkative: the sober with the gluttonous, the fervent with the lukewarm; the studious with the idle; the interior with the extern: the simple with the cunning, the truthful with the guileful; the provident with the careless, the learned with the ignorant; the prudent with the foolish, the strong with the weak: the constant with the instable, the modest with the wrangling: and so of many other vices and manners of men good and bad, according to that of Isaias the prophet: "The wolf shall dwell with the lamb; and the leopard shall lie down with the kid; the calf and the lion and the sheep shall abide together: and a little child shall lead them." But all these things both prosperous and contrary happen with the good and the bad alike in this life by divine permission: to manifest the secret judgements of God in all His ways: that the elect may be proved and the devout purified by means of the wicked; and may not take pride in the good things bestowed on them. The bad live with the good, that by the example of the good they may be aroused to the amendment of their morals: and may not have excuse through ignorance of good life and discipline: which they see in the good associated with them. Some are very inconstant: and are soon moved to hatred or love, by a slight word or action of another. They laugh for a frivolous story; and they are angry for a passing fly. Some for recreation seek men: and lose God and the saints. It is not a slight loss: to lose the grace of devotion through over-much talking. Some speak of the ill deeds of others: and neglect to correct their own shortcomings. Some speak beforehand of future wars upon earth: but it were better that they thought of the wars against vice and how to overcome them. If eternal goods and evils were taken to heart: all things of time would speedily vanish away. Those who are of the world speak of the world; and those who love Christ, think of heavenly things: and willingly discourse to others the heavenly things which they love. The foolish narrate things foolish and vain: and the light of heart willingly listen to frivolities. It is good, therefore, to be silent concerning frivolous things and uncertain happenings; and to commit to God all His secret judgements: without Whose Providence not even the leaf of a tree falls to the ground. Not without cause is the just oppressed: or the poor man robbed: or the guiltless slain. No man has wherewith justly to complain of God: for He disposes all things justly, wisely and providently: although Man does not understand the ways of His justice.

For he who strongly sets his hope in God, stands well and shall not waver: however things may befall in this world. From whence then contentions and wars amongst men? Are they not from the concupiscence of the flesh and pride of the spirit? For the desire of money is the root of all evils. Which if it be not restrained: leads to innumerable ills. For when the good things desired are refused, or possessed are taken away: the soul becomes sad, the hidden passion of strife rises in the heart: and anger appears upon the countenance, and a hard word breaks from the mouth. In us then is the material of strife and the hotbed of discord; to wit, the desire of a thing, love of possessing, fear of losing, grief for a good lost. But the wicked and impatient man hurts himself more than others: and is harmed more by himself within, than by others without. Every passionate man is a burden to himself and a disturbance of heart: wherever he may be, whether alone or with many others. A constant and domestic strife is this of ours: for our flesh is not subject to the spirit according to the right reason of a good life; nor is the spirit perfectly submissive to God: according to His every will to please Him alone within, here and for ever. But the malicious devil cannot rest: and where he does not come himself, he sends a messenger secretly: to disturb the peace of others, or cunningly deceive them. For he either withdraws from good, or urges to evil: or suggests false for true: or makes the true doubtful. But he is deceived who believes him. What else has he to do: but to run about through the world and tempt men, and annoy the good? But those who trust in God, and speedily have recourse to prayer: are able by the help of Christ to break all his designs as spiders" webs: and ought to fear in naught the threats of the wicked. No one is more safe from the snares of temptations than the truly humble, the perfectly obedient, and poor pilgrim; who seeks no earthly ease: nor desires the goods of the world. Who is he and we will truly praise him? O how praiseworthy a virtue is humility: which escapes all the nets of the devil. How precious and beautiful the virtue of chastity: which overcomes the seductions of the flesh with all the pomps of the world. A great virtue is voluntary poverty: whereby Heaven is bought without money. A noble virtue patience: by which are overcome all the adversities of the world. A sublime virtue obedience: to which are often subject the elements and things that seem impossible to men.

AN EXAMPLE OF OBEDIENCE

There was a certain devout Prioress in the Order of Regulars once very ill of a fever. Compassionating whose sufferings a young sister even shed tears. Who secretly entering the choir, casting herself before the relics of the saints, prayed earnestly, that the mother might be cured: and she stricken with fever in her stead. And straightway so it was. For, her prayer finished, the young maiden began to be ill: and the Prioress the same day and subsequently recovered. But the most loving mother hearing that the young one is ill: called her, asking from her what she had done or eaten. Who answered: "I have eaten nothing evil. But I thought and asked the Lord that it would be better that I should be sick for you: and you should be well." Then the devout mother with the good hope which she had in God said: "On the part of God I command thee by obedience: that thou be sick no longer." And God hearing their prayers, gave them both health to the invocation, praise and honour of His name. Amen.

AN EXAMPLE OF PATIENCE

A certain Brother questioned a pilgrim coming from afar, saying: "Tell me, good friend, what good things have you heard and seen on the way?" He answered: "I have heard the patience of the poor praised enough by many: but I have seen it imitated by few." "What more?" He said. "Amid delights I have found thorns; amid honours I have seen sorrows: and amid riches I have frequently found strifes, and great anxieties." "Is anyone free from these ills?" Quoth he, sadly. "Very few in these days. And if there are many: I do not know them. Happy, therefore, the religious, who know how to be content with a little: and desire to be honoured, or praised by no man. For God shall be their reward. For seldom do I come across such an one, as does not grieve for his own loss: or complain for his neighbour. However, if peace is to be hoped for anywhere in this life: then the truly humble has it: who patiently bears wrongs and holds his peace." He therefore who wishes to have peace, and a good conscience; let him forsake his own will for the love of God: and learn patiently to endure the injustice and contempt of men. For thus did Christ bearing for us the shameful cross: and obeying the Father even unto death.

PART III

SERMON XX

OF DAILY TAKING UP THE CROSS EMBRACED IN RELIGION

GOD forbid that I should glory: save in the Cross of Our Lord Jesus Christ. Beloved brethren, blessed Paul the glorious beholder of heavenly secrets, shows us in the above words of the holy cross, the right path of a good life; a most excellent doctrine for bearing adversity: a most firm ladder to rise to Heaven by the ever unconquered sign of the holy cross. For this leads its lovers into the country of eternal light, of eternal peace and eternal bliss; which the world cannot give, nor the devil take away. Human weakness dreads to suffer poverty, abjection, lowliness, hunger, toil, pain, distress, mockery, which things often befall, and grieve and disturb a man: but all these things joined together, sent to us by a dispensation of God, form a saving cross by manifold suffering: and open to true cross-bearers, who take up their cross, the gate of the heavenly kingdom, make ready the palm of life for them that combat: and bestow on the conquerors the crown of everlasting glory.

O truly blessed cross of Christ, which hast merited to bear the King of Heaven: and hast brought the joy of salvation to the whole world. By thee the devils are routed, the sick are healed: the fearful are comforted, the vicious are purified, the slothful are aroused; the proud are humbled, the hard are touched: and the devout are watered with tears. Blessed those who daily recall the Passion of Christ: and desire to carry their cross after Christ. Good and religious brothers standing under obedience in daily affliction of the body and in resignation of their own will have now a cross outwardly hard and bitter; but within full of sweetness: because of the hope of eternal salvation, and the inflowing of divine consolation promised to the troubled of heart. And if they do not constantly feel this, or find that it comes but slowly; nevertheless they must await with patience: and abandon themselves to the divine will. For He knows best the time for mercy and the manner of succouring the distressed: as a physician knows the art of healing: and a master the skill of ruling and the hour for reading. Interior bearers of the cross have great confidence and reason for glorying in the cross of Jesus Christ; for they do not trust and presume to be saved of their own merits and works: but of the mercy of God and the merits of Jesus Christ crucified for our sins; in Whom they faithfully believe, and heartily love: Whom they confess with the mouth, praise, preach, honour, and bless.

God is wont is prove His familiar friends by the holy cross whether they truly or feignedly seek and love Him: and whether they perfectly keep His commandments. But they are especially proved by the sufferance of wrongs, and the withdrawal of interior consolations: by the death of friends and the loss of things: by achings of the head and injuries of the limbs: by abstinence from food and coarseness of attire; by the hardness of bed and coldness of feet; by long watchings at night, and labours by day: by silence of the mouth, and the corrections of superiors: by biting worms and detracting tongues. But amidst these things they are comforted by devout meditation on the Lord's Passion: as it has been in secret made manifest to many devout. For it is theirs to taste the honey hidden in the rock: and the oil of mercy distilling from the blessed wood of the holy cross: whose savour is most excellent, odour most sweet, touch most wholesome, fruit most happy. O truly most worthy and most precious tree of life, planted in the midst of the Church for the healing of the soul. O Jesus of Nazareth crucified; Thou dost loose the chains of sinners: dost free the souls of the saints, dost humble the necks of the proud: dost crush the might of the wicked, dost strengthen the faithful: dost put unbelievers to flight, dost lift up the pious; dost scourge the obstinate, dost overcome our foes: dost raise up the bruised, dost deliver the oppressed; dost strike the guilty, dost protect the innocent: dost love the truthful, dost hate the lying; dost despise the carnal, dost regard the spiritual: dost receive them that come to Thee, dost conceal them that flee to Thee. Thou dost hear them that call upon Thee: dost rejoice them that visit Thee; dost aid them that seek Thee: dost comfort them that cry to Thee. Thou honourest them that honour Thee: praisest them that praise Thee; lovest them that love Thee: glorifiest them that worship Thee; blessest them that bless Thee: exaltest them that exalt Thee: Thou lookest on them that look to Thee: kissest them that kiss Thee: embracest them that embrace Thee: leadest them to Heaven that follow Thee.

But woe to the lovers of the world, who do not heed the footsteps of Christ: nor walk by the way of the holy cross; but to fulfil their desires: heap up gold and silver: which they can by no means carry with them. Wo to the proud and great in their own eyes: who spurn the humility of the devout, deride simplicity: call poverty misery, make little account of obedience; drive patience from them, keep chastity ill: and live in a manner contrary to the Crucified. Wo to the nice and particular, who nurse their flesh too much and adorn it outwardly with raiment: and neglect their soul and stain it with sins. Wo to the avaricious and ambitious; who for earthly goods and honours labour much and often quarrel: and for heavenly goods and everlasting joys are able to do and suffer little. Therefore they often on a sudden lose the things of earth: and they gain not those of Heaven. For no man can rejoice here with the world: and reign there with Christ crucified for us. The servant is not greater than his lord nor the disciple above his master: Whom it behoved to suffer the cross, and so enter into His glory And assuredly after the most fleeting joys of this life: follow eternal lamentations. And then they shall be cruelly tormented in fire and sulphur: who now eat daintily and plentifully: and drink wine with laughter and pleasure. except you do penance." saith the Lord: "you shall all likewise perish."

There are mortal men who do not consider their fraility nor think of the baseness of the clay whence they were made: but glory in the nobility of their race: swell with pride over wealthy parents, are puffed up for their knowledge and art, presume of their strength and beauty: exult in power and place, are lifted up because of their ornate and diversified garments: rejoice in the publicity and fame of their name, take pleasure in the visits of friends; are saddened at the loss of their honour: are tortured at the success and promotion of others their rivals. But alas, all these things carefully examined and truly weighed: are vain, and worth no esteem: for suddenly they shall fail, and be reduced to nothing. sooth all flesh is grass; and all worldly state falls as the flower of the field, withers and rots: and becomes as if it had never been here.

There are also many others intent on vain amusements, at variance with the sign of Christ's cross: and far removed in their ways and actions from the fellowship of the saints. Who as if mad rejoice in the various shows of the world, in psalteries and citherns, bugles and organs: run and dance with their feet, clap with their hands: sing with their voices, laugh with their teeth; and for merriment of heart scarcely contain themselves in the motions of their body: because they set their supreme good in present amusements and pleasures. Which if it were lasting and acceptable to God: would be very desirable and praiseworthy. But, alas, how greatly men are deceived, both kings and princes of the people: rejoicing in the vanities of this world. For vanity is every man living, passing as a shadow: and as the dew that goeth away in the morning. O how far these are from the supreme good, from the sweetness of God, from the melodies of the angels: from the paths of the just, from the holiness of religious: and from the spiritual joy of the devout. It shall come, it shall come speedily upon them, death, before they know it, who now rejoice as if they were safe: and all amusements and song shall cease in their houses and streets. And the poor shall rejoice, and the weak and despised of this world, with all true crossbearers, lovers of Christ: who have crcuified their flesh with the vices and concupiscences in this world: that they may not be condemned with the wicked in the judgement to come.

Wo also to wandering and dissipated monks, religious only in name and habit; who carry their cross with murmuring and obey unwillingly: keep their cell ill, easily break silence; shun toil, love idleness: shorten prayers, lengthen gossip: ready for exterior things, slow to interior; drowsy in meditating good things, inclined to think of evil: cheerful for eating and drinking, sorry to fast: easy in finding fault, weak for endurance; desirous of honours, ashamed of things lowly: disliking strictness of discipline, and always inclined to greater laxity. But alack, good God, that the children of this world are more prudent and eager in acquiring, increasing and preserving earthly things: than the children of light and the servants of the holy cross in gathering virtues and rooting out vices. O would that all would be wise and understand how delightful it is to be engaged in devout exercises, to search the hidden things of scripture: to meditate the words and works of Christ, often to read, often to pray, to ponder the things read and heard; daily to recall the favours of God: for all good gifts and creatures, even for the least to give thanks to God; ever to aim at better things, to sigh for heavenly: and to drive far from the heart all the things of earth. Of how holy it is to stand in careful guard over the heart: to shut out wanderings by fervent prayer and pure meditation; to conquer the imagery of the world by the image of the crucified: to drive away the temptations of the devil with the holy cross, the nails, and the lance: to quench the motions of the flesh with thorns and cutting scourges; to bear wrongs done with a patient soul, to reckon losses and reproaches a gain to the soul: and all present burdens to weigh as most light for the love of Christ. For attentively to think of these things and the like, and to strive to put them in practice, is to take up the cross: and to glory in the cross of Christ, and not in the flesh. For from the sweet wood of the cross, a sweet odour of heavenly grace breathes; which drives away all worldly joys, quenches all delights of the flesh: keeps down elation of the heart, brings the gifts of interior comfort to the sad; affords strength to them that suffer wrong: calms anxious souls in divers ways by the words and examples of Christ.

O religious brother, why art thou sad and complainest of the weight of thy cross in long watchings, in many fasts, in toil and silence, in obedience and severe discipline: which have been profitably instituted by the holy fathers under the inspiration of God for thy progress and salvation of soul; that thou mayest walk thereby in safety and prudence: who canst not well and virtuously govern thyself. Dost think that thou in preference to all the saints shalt enter the kingdom of heaven without the cross and sorrow: a thing which Christ neither could nor would, and which none of His dearest friends and saints obtained? For He Himself said: "Christ ought to suffer: and so enter into His glory." Thou art certainly mistaken in thy judgement: nor dost thou heed Christ's footsteps shown to thee: Who by the cross passed from this world to His heavenly Father. Ask any one of the conquerors and citizens of the heavenly kingdom: how he came to possess for ever this glory of God. Was it not through the cross and suffering? Ah, beloved brethren, take the yoke of the Lord upon you, sweet and light to them that love; embrace with desire the holy cross flourishing in all virtues, full of heavenly unction: that it may lead you securely with the hope of glory unto life everlasting. What more do you want? This is the way and no other; the straight way, the holy way, the perfect way: the way of Christ, the way of the just, the way of the chosen ones who are to be saved. Walk therein, persevere therein; endure therein, live therein: die therein, expire therein. The cross of Christ overcomes all the wiles of the devil: the cross draws to it the hearts of all the faithful; the cross destroys all evils, and bestows upon us all goods: through Jesus Christ Who hung and died thereon. There is no armour so strong nor arrow so keen and terrible against the power and fury of the devil, which he fears so much as the sign of the holy cross: whereon he made the Son of God to be hanged and slain: Who was guiltless and pure of all blemish. O truly blessed cross of Christ most worthy of all honour, to be embraced with all love, to lovers light unto bearing burdens, to the sad comforting unto the endurance of reproaches, to the penitent indulgent unto the remission of debts for all offences. This is to the holy angels very honourable; to men very loveable, to demons most terrible, despised of the proud, acceptable to the humble: hard to the carnal, sweet to the spiritual, tasteless to the foolish, tender to the devout, affable to the poor, companionable to the wayfarer, friendly to the afflicted, consoling to the sick, comforting to the dying. Store up then in the secret place of your heart all the sacred wounds of Jesus; which savour above all spices to the devout soul living in grief: and not seeking outwardly solace from men. Weigh also the sorrows of the blessed virgin Mother of Jesus standing by the cross; how many tears she then shed to intimate compassion with the many women weeping with her: that she also may be mindful of you in your distresses. Follow Christ by His Passion and cross which lead to eternal rest and light; for if now you are the companions of His tribulation: you shall hereafter be with Him fellows of the heavenly table and everlasting exultation.

Plant in the little garden of your memory the tree of the holy cross: bearing a powerful medicine against all the fatal suggestions of the devil. For the root of this most noble and most happy tree is humility and poverty: its bark toil and penance: its branches mercy and justice: its leaves truth and doctrine: its flowers probity and modesty: its odour, temperance and abstinence; its beauty, chastity and obedience: its glory, a right faith and a strong hope: its strength, magnanimity and patience: its length, longanimity and perseverance: its breadth, gentleness and concord: its height, charity and wisdom: its sweetness love and joy, its fruit salvation and life eternal. Well therefore and worthily in holy Church is it sung of the sacred cross: that no wood produces such a tree, full of leaf, flower, seed. Yea, not even in the gardens of Solomon is found such a kind, nor a herb so powerful for the remedy of every sickness: as the tree of the holy cross bearing spices of divine virtue unto the restoration of man's salvation. This is the most fruitful tree, blessed above all the trees of Paradise; reaching out with most beautiful branches, adorned with green leaves: extended through the world in its most abundant fruits; touching the heavens with its height: penetrating hell with its depth: in its breadth embracing mountains and hills: in its greatness filling the whole earth: in its strength overcoming wicked kings and persecutors of the faith: in its piety drawing the feeble, in its sweetness healing sinners. This is the God-bearing vine, the fruitful olive: the sweet fig-tree, rough without, as honey within; planted in the house of God, rooted in humility, proved in patience: consummated in obedience, confirmed in charity. This is the beautiful palm, worthily called the Christ-bearer, borne on the shoulder of Jesus, raised on high on Mount Calvary; condemned by the Jews, defaced by the Gentiles: insulted by the wicked, denied by the faithless; lamented by the faithful, invoked by the pious: much loved by the devout, supremely reverenced by the religious. This was shown from Heaven to the Emperor Constantine: diligently sought by the holy queen Helena: and found with great joy. This was lovingly embraced by the same noble worshipper of Christ, watered with a tearful face: and most affectionately kissed with pure lips. This now by the marvellous dispensation of God in many places is resplendent with signs and powers: this is adored, sought and honoured by kings and princes of the world, by all the clergy and people: and is worshipped and reverenced with greater devotion by all the faithful of Christ for all the wounds and insults wrought it by the wicked. Nevertheless, by the hidden design and providence of God: all these things were done and ordained for the salvation of the world. This often touches the devout soul with the affection of pious compassion: often makes the tears flow when she looks upon the image of the Crucified: often wounds the heart of the lover, when he thinks of Christ wounded for him. Happy man and faithful servant he: who constantly bears the sacred wounds of Jesus in his heart: and whatever adversity befalls him, accepts it from the hand of God and patiently endures: that he may be made like to the Crucified, at least in a little. For he is worthy to be visited and consoled by Christ: who endeavours to conform himself fully to His Passion in life and in death. This is the way of the holy cross, this the teaching of our Saviour; this the wisdom of the saints, this the rule of monks, this the life of the good: this the reading of clerics, this the meditation of the devout, humbly to imitate Christ: for Christ to suffer ills, to take bitter for sweet: to spurn honours, equably to endure contempt: to abstain from evil pleasures, to shun occasions of vice, to avoid dissipations: to mourn for his own and others' shortcomings, to pray for the afflicted and tempted: to rejoice over them that do well, to sympathize with them that endure wrongs, to succour the needy; not to desire lofty things, to choose the lowly, to love the simple: to cut off the superfluous, to be content with little: to labour for virtue, to struggle daily against vice: to master the flesh by fast, to strengthen the spirit by prayer and reading: to refuse human praise, to seek solitude, to love silence: to take leisure in God, to sigh for heavenly things: to despise from the heart all earthly things: to deem nothing his comfort besides God. This one is able to say with blessed Paul the apostle: "For to me to live is Christ, and to die is gain." And again: "It behoves me to glory in the cross of my Lord Jesus Christ: by whom this world is crucified to me and I to the world." O religious monk and follower of a strict life: do not depart from the cross embraced in the Order; but bear and carry the cross even unto death: and thou shalt find eternal rest, heavenly honour and glory. When any trouble befalls thee, then Christ meets thee with the cross: and shows thee the way by which thou shouldst go to the heavenly kingdom. But if a man glories and hopes in the wealth and honours of this world, truly he is deceived: and he shall carry nothing with him of all the things that he was wont to love in the world. But he who glories in the cross of Christ and despises all things for Christ's sake: he again shall be comforted by Christ now: and hereafter he shall be filled with heavenly goods: and without end with Christ and all the saints shall most happily rejoice. Which may Jesus Christ deign to grant us, Who suffered on the cross and died for us: to Whom be eternal praise and glory for ever and ever. Amen.

AN EXAMPLE CONCERNING THE HOLY CROSS

There was with us a certain laic named Nicholas Peters: born in the country of Holland. He by the inspiration of God resolved in his soul to leave the world, although he was a good carpenter: and to enter our monastery. When therefore he was alone in the way and was coming near the monastery: by the snares and temptation of the devil he commenced to be anxious and to be much afraid: without knowing what was opposing him in the good road, while the sun was still shining brightly. Standing therefore and asking himself what he should do, when he saw that there was nobody there: he began to think that perhaps the devil wanted to hinder him: to prevent him going on further to the monastery. Looking round therefore on this side and on that, he saw at a distance as it were a little black cloud rise from the earth, and gradually grow bigger and higher: and move as if driven by the wind. Being therefore very much frightened, and guessing that Satan was striving to obstruct his path, that he might not fulfil his purpose: at once raising his hand he made the sign of the holy cross: and armed his forehead with the saving sign. And so casting away fear and strengthened in a strong faith: again signing his forehead with the cross he went forward bravely. And when he had done this, that diabolical phantasy not being able to endure the power of the holy cross, and as if shunning a sharp arrow shot against it, turned aside from the path: and soon vanishing like smoke entirely disappeared. Then made very joyful he boldly entered our monastery dedicated in honour of St. Agnes virgin: which commencing at that time in great poverty was known to few. Living here many years after this, in honour of the holy cross he fasted every Friday: and even when wearied with great labours at harvest time, he never dispensed the fast of the holy cross: but most constantly fulfilled his purpose, which he had well commenced.

ANOTHER

There was a certain Lay-sister by name Margaret devout to God in the Order of Sisters Regular: who, assigned to the office of cook as a faithful Martha: strove to serve Christ and the sisters humbly, as long as she was able. On one occasion then a pan of oil had been placed over the fire which was burning: and she busied with her work was not far away. And when she saw that the oil was boiling too much and its froth rising high: fearing that it would spill and be consumed by the fire: she ran quickly to the stove. And when she had made the sign of the holy cross over it; at once the swelling of the froth subsided to the bottom: as if she had thrown cold water in. Seeing which her companion marvelled; and afterwards made known this fact to others.

ANOTHER

A certain woman of Kempen went to the town market: to buy herself and her servants a little milk. Having bought it, she hastened to return home: holding in her hand the milk jug which she had brought with her. While on the way then, she felt a desire to drink of the milk: and bending down she sat upon the ground. And so taking the jug in her hand, she made on herself the sign of the cross before she should drink; and at once the jug cracked at the bottom: and the milk escaping to the ground flowed out in streams. Seeing this, very much terrified she arose; and thinking over what marvel had befallen her: by this she clearly recognized the power of the holy cross. And some hearing what had happened: said: "Perhaps if this woman had not signed herself with the sign of the holy cross: she would have drunk in the devil with the milk." It is good therefore first to bless food and drink with the sign of the holy cross: lest any evil befall a man from the vice of gluttony, by which the devil too often tempts and takes many captive.

ANOTHER

Two religious Brothers having received leave were walking together not far beyond the monastery gate: to return after an hour to their cell the friend of devotion. While therefore they were talking together of different topics pleasing to them: there chimed in also from want of watchfulness over the mouth a word of detraction concerning the actions of their Prior by the instigation of the malevolent spirit. Then suddenly there appeared to them a black horse very terrible coming with speed towards them in their walk: and as if wishing to rush upon them as they conversed. And they, dreadfully afraid, at once arming themselves with the sign of the holy cross, with hastened steps fled to the monastery gate: and thus escaped the danger of the most fierce enemy by the sign of the holy cross. And they said: "We have done ill: speaking idle and detracting words of others. Therefore so dreadful a monster came upon us: that we may be on our guard in future against the most wicked sin of detraction hateful to all."

ANOTHER

A certain brother wearied out with labour, when late in the evening he set himself to sleep: neglected to sign himself as usual with the sign of the holy cross against the fear of the foe. For overcome quickly by sleep: he did not arm himself with the sign of the saving cross. Afterwards he was so terribly frightened in his sleep by the old enemy of the human race: that he cried out with a loud voice for fear: and awakening trembled with great wonder. Then he remembered that on the previous evening he had not signed himself with sufficient care with the accustomed standard of the holy cross: and therefore the malevolent foe was so savagely troublesome to him that night. Returning therefore fully to himself, having called upon the saving name of Jesus, he signed himself with the cross; and devoutly recited the prayer of the holy cross: and so falling asleep again, he rested securely in the peace of Christ. And on account of this happening through the sign of the holy cross: he thinks that no place of the world is safe from the terror of the enemy without the cross of Christ.

ANOTHER

A certain good man saw in a dream the image of the holy cross standing near him. And first it stood before him and faced him: but afterwards standing behind him it struck him on the back and departed. Being much terrified and puzzled over this: he made known to a certain devout priest what he had seen. Who weighing the vision and not thinking it vain: said to the troubled man: "Perhaps Our Lord wishes to try you: and to put some burden on you to bear. You should make ready then your back to bear the cross lovingly with Him: for He scourges every son whom He loveth." With these words the man was consoled, trusting himself to God: Who does naught except for the best. And not long afterwards, there came upon him tribulation and the contempt of men: which the cross seen before in sleep foreshadowed. But he being carefully forewarned disposed himself to patience: and after a worthy trial he closed his life with a good end.

ANOTHER

A certain devout Brother strove to exercise himself in the Lord's Passion in preference to the other sacred books: and held the image of the holy cross in great veneration. And wherever he saw a cross, humbly bowing he took pleasure in signing himself +: mindful of his God crucified for him, Whom he desired to love and honour. One night then he saw in a vision a certain image of the holy cross hanging on the wall of a certain church: most cruelly torn with many wounds and blows. And looking upon it with exceeding great sorrow: with bowed knees and joined hands he suppliantly worshipped. And at once the image stretched out to him its right arm from the cross: and offered him its right hand. And while he wondered much at such great condescension: it was said to him: "This for the honour which thou hast shown Me on the cross." Thenceforth a very great devotion commenced to grow in his heart towards the image of the holy cross: and it became very sweet to him daily to meditate, read and pray on the Passion of the Lord.

A PRAYER OF PRAISE OF THE HOLY CROSS

O most sweet and most loving cross of my Lord Jesus Christ, exceedingly sad and bitter without: but within full of divine sweetness. O tree beautiful and bright: adorned with the members of Christ as with precious jewels. O fruitful vine: pierced with cruel nails. O lovely olive, coloured with the blood of Christ: hallowed by the water of His side. O tree of life: bearing the King of glory for the salvation of the world. O cross, impregnable buckler, incomparable standard of the King, admirable symbol of salvation: on the title-head having this writing: Jesus of Nazareth the King of the Jews. Hail Jesus of Nazareth, praise of the angels, life of the blessed: pardon of sinners, salvation of all the peoples. O saving cross foreseen and chosen from eternity: thou art beautified with the flowers of all virtues, thou art worthily worshipped: thou art resplendent with miracles, thou aboundest in fruits of eternal salvation: thou art redolent above all spices, thou dost heal diseases of body and soul: thou dost open Heaven to the just, thou dost bring forgiveness to sinners; thou dost rout the devil, thou dost crush hell: thou dost free captives, thou dost beatify the redeemed. O cross, tree most glorious, blessed above all the woods of the groves; thou art more lofty than the cedar, more wide-spreading than the palm, more fragrant than the cypress, more noble than the balsam, more fruitful than the vine, more rich than the olive: more sweet than the fig, more fresh than the box, stronger than the oak: more lovely than the rose, whiter than the lily. O cross most brilliant, higher than the sun, brighter than the stars, purer than the moon: more sparkling than gems, more precious than stones, more valuable than gold, better than silver, more efficacious than the spiknard, more wholesome than all spices and medicines.

O cross most lovable, supremely venerable: be to me a sinner kind and propitious: the guide of a good life, the light of a right path; a defender from the foe; a deliverer in the awful judgement: and a loving welcomer into the kingdom above. Assist me in my agony, strengthen me in faith, grant hope of pardon, pour charity into my heart: and grant me to pass with a happy end from this world: that through thee He may receive me, Who hung on thee and redeemed me: Jesus Christ our Lord: Who with the Father.

The world praises its lovers, its mighty soldiers and barons: who have fought for their fatherland and citizens; and have manfully exposed themselves to many dangers and death: and have set the common good before all private and peculiar interests; how much more is Christ to be praised and loved Who for us all was crucified and died: that we might live for ever and reign with Him in Heaven. Amen.

SERMON XXI

OF THE VENERATION AND COMMEMORATION OF THE BLESSED VIRGIN MARY

THERE stood by the cross of Jesus His Mother. Beloved brethren, it is meet and in due order that after the commemoration of the holy cross, we have a special commemoration also of the grief of the most blessed ever Virgin Mother of God Mary: who faithfully stood by her beloved Son Jesus hanging on the cross: and dying for the salvation of the whole world. O tearful spectacle of the mother and the crucified Son; the mother weeping and the Son compassionating: the mother fainting and the Son addressing; the mother standing under the cross and the Son hanging on the cross: the mother sighing, and the Son expiring. O greatness of boundless sorrow, never to be forgotten: but firmly to be held in the hearts of the devout. Pilate wrote a title, on the tablet above the cross: Jesus of Nazareth the King of the Jews. Write thou also the same title in thy heart in letters of gold against the mockery of men and the terrors of the demons: and Christ the King of Heaven shall free thee from all the violence of the wicked. If thou dost so the Mother of Jesus Mary will stand by thee also with her prayers: that thou mayest not lose heart in thy anguish and distress. For no mother had so great a joy and comfort in the birth of her child, as this most blessed one experienced: who merited to conceive and bring forth the Son of God. No mother also had and endured so great a sadness and unbearable a grief in the death of her child according to the flesh: as this most loving Mother felt from compassion in the Passion of her most dear Son: when she stood by His cross, and pierced through with the sword of sorrow wept most bitterly. Assuredly having beheld such pains in the Son, Whom she loved alone beyond measure above all things: it was most wonderful, that she could live longer in the body: whose soul the sword of sorrow transpierced as often: as she saw or heard her Son tormented and mocked. O truly singular martyrdom in the desolate Mother and tender Virgin: who was more cruelly tortured in her heart compassionating her Son: than any martyr hanging on the rack.

Brothers, if you love Our Lady and desire her patronage in every distress: then stand with her by the cross of Jesus compassionating her and her beloved Son from your inmost heart: that she also in turn may earnestly pray for your sins and negligences in death. For he who now thinks over and weighs with pious affection of mind often and devoutly the Lord's Passion and the tears of His most grief-stricken Mother; should hope of the mercy of God, and the kindness of both Mother and Son that they will be by him also in his need: and succour him with consolation when he lies in his last agony.

O how joyful will that soul be, which loved Jesus and Mary in its life: and every day turned over in mind the sorrowful standing of Mary by the cross of Jesus. Happy that religious who despising all the comforts of the world: has taken unto himself Our Lady St. Mary as his comforting Mother: and the protecting guardian of his whole life. Let no man doubt that the gentle and pitiful Mother, the consoler of the poor, and the helper of orphans, will willingly speak for her faithful servant setting out from this world a word good and sweet: appeasing the face of her beloved Son our Redeemer by her holy prayers, saying: "O my most loving Son have mercy on the soul of Thy servant who has loved and praised me, as Thou well knowest and hast seen: from whose mouth the holy angels have very often brought me the pleasure of a devout salutation: who also was wont to invite many brothers to praise with him Thy holy name and mine. He is our secretary writing sacred books and a lover of the holy cross: willingly praying and chanting psalms: who on hearing Thy name and mine was wont reverently to bow to us: and to greet us bending the knee. Passing by the way and seeing at a distance the cross: mindful of Thy Passion, he showed Thee reverence, bowing to the cross. Also when he beheld in a church or in any place my image painted or Thee lying or seated on my lap, or hanging as dead in my arms: at once he was moved with compassion and grieved, wept and prayed: bowed his knees and worshipped. He never left us without a kiss of love: but all the day and night he hid in his heart the sorrows of Thy holy wounds and the weeping of my eyes: and from his inmost soul strove to compassionate me. Be mindful then of these things, my most dear Son; and grant him now to find mercy in Thy sight: while I with great urgency beseech for him with all Thy angels and saints."

Brothers, you ought to give heed to these things now while you are in health: and have time for amendment. You should procure for yourselves now such friends and advocates to speak a good word very acceptable to God for your trespasses and debts: and to receive you into their eternal dwellings, after the dangers and toilsome struggles of this world. For you will not find more faithful friends and more powerful in Heaven and on earth: than Jesus the King of angels and Mary Our Lady the Queen of Heaven. If you are lovers of Christ, take up the cross of Christ, follow the cross: stand near the cross, embrace the cross, forsake not the cross: until you come to Jesus Christ, the true light, Who saith: "I am the light of the world: he that followeth Me, walketh not in darkness." If you seek to be consoled in every tribulation: draw nigh to Mary the Mother of Jesus standing by the cross, weeping and sorrowing: and all your burdens will either speedily depart: or become more bearable. Choose this most kind Mother of Jesus in preference to all your relatives and friends as your special mother and advocate before death; and greet her frequently with the angelic salutation: for she loves very much to hear this word. If the malignant enemy tempts you and hinders from the praise of God and Mary: care not nor cease to praise and pray; but so much the more earnestly invoke Mary, salute Mary: think of Mary, call Mary by her name. Honour Mary, ever glorify Mary: bow to Mary, commend yourselves to Mary. With Mary abide in your cell: with Mary keep silence: with Mary rejoice: with Mary sorrow. With Mary toil: with Mary watch: with Mary pray: with Mary walk: with Mary sit. With Mary seek Jesus: with Mary bear Jesus in your arms: with Mary and Jesus dwell in Nazareth. With Mary go to Jerusalem: with Mary stand by the cross of Jesus; with Mary weep for Jesus: with Mary bury Jesus. With Mary and Jesus rise; with Mary and Jesus go up to Heaven: with Mary and Jesus desire to live and die. Brothers, if you think over and practise these things well: the devil will flee from you: and you will make progress in the spiritual life. Mary will willingly pray for you for her clemency: and Jesus will willingly hear His Mother for her reverence. It is little that we do: but if we approach the Father through Mary and Jesus her Son with a humble and contrite heart: we shall obtain mercy and grace in this time: and glory hereafter with them without end. Amen. Happy the devout soul which has Jesus and Mary as familiar friends in this life: comrades at table, companions on the way: providers in need, comforters in tribulation: helpers in danger, counsellors in doubt: welcomers at the end. Happy the religious who deems himself a pilgrim in this world: and for his sovereign solace has Jesus and Mary in the guest-house of his heart.

Examples concerning the Angelic Salutation

AN EXAMPLE

A certain brother lost a little book in his cell: and after searching carefully a long time he could not find it. And while he grieved at its loss and gave up hope of finding it: he turned himself to prayer, calling upon the Blessed Virgin by the angelic salutation. When therefore he had commenced to recite as usual the Hail Mary and had repeated the same often, and meanwhile thought with sorrow of the little book: of a sudden there came into his mind this inspiration: as he sat near the bed praying before a picture of the Blessed Virgin Mary. "Seek here before thee under the straw of the bed." At once he stretched out his hand to the bedstead: wishing to try whether anything was hidden there. And lo, lifting the straw a little: he soon touched the book with his hand and drew it forth. And seeing it he wondered, and kissing the little book for joy, he gave thanks to God: and hastened to pay the Blessed Virgin the angelic salutations promised her. And he said: "Perchance Our Lady wanted to have some Hail Marys: and therefore thou couldst not find the little book so soon." It is good then often to recite the Hail Mary: and devoutly to call upon the Mother of Jesus.

ANOTHER

A certain brother writing books in his cell: by the wiles of the devil was troubled with a bad thought. Feeling this and being angry with it, he rose at once, to go out of his cell: and escape this annoyance more speedily. But before he went out, by an inspiration from God he looked at a picture of the Blessed Virgin, which he had by him: and was wont to greet out of devotion. And so at once he knelt down: and with joined hands began devoutly to recite the Hail Mary. And lo, divine grace came to his aid at once; our loving Lady Mary succouring him: with her noble blessed offspring. For having commenced and recited attentively the angel salutation; when at the end he had said, Jesus Christ, Amen: immediately he felt within him the power of God, and peace from all disturbance. Astounded therefore at the speedy answer to his prayer: he recognized in this instance, the great utility of the angelic salutation: against every assault of the enemy whatsoever. And giving thanks to God, he said within himself: "Now I know truly: that Our Lady St. Mary is mighty to aid and deliver all that cry to her." But on the following night: this vision appeared to him in his sleep. For it seemed to him, that he was passing alone through the orchard. And Satan coming towards him: commenced to terrify him and drive him back. And he frightened from his face: began to run, to escape his hands. And as he did not dare to go outside the monastery bounds: from his hasty running he suddenly fell into a ditch of water into the mud at the bottom. Fearing therefore to be drowned since he saw nobody there to help him and draw him out: he began to recite the angelic salutation within himself and to pray for aid. And as soon as he had said Jesus Christ, Amen: he was snatched out of the deep pool of water, and set again upon dry land. Then being made exceedingly joyful, and as if delivered from the snare of death: he awakened and came fully to himself. Raising himself therefore on his bed, he began to weep for joy: and in thanksgiving he recited with attention very many times on bended knees the Hail Mary. He added also these words: "Hail sweet Mary Our Lady full of grace: the Lord is with thee gate of mercy."

ANOTHER

Two brothers Regular were going together to the upper country: for the pious purpose of visiting relatives and friends faithful in Christ. It befell them therefore to wander a little from the right path. And so the elder said to the younger. "Brother, it seems to me we are going out of our way: let us return again to the high road." Returning then to where they were before, the senior began to pray and to call upon the Blessed Virgin: to send them a guide for the right way, and a traveller of good companionship. And while he was now reciting some prayers with hymns and collects of the Blessed Virgin: behold there came towards them a certain man in the guise of a pilgrim, carrying with him a staff and a satchel on his back for provision on the way. And having greeted the brothers: he said that he was going up country to St. Quirinus for the indulgences, and that he would willingly accompany them. Quickly therefore they followed this guide of the right way for the space of a long journey: until they came to the wished-for place of their lodging. Then the elder recognizing that divine help had come to them, strove to render most ample thanks to God and the Blessed Virgin for the guidance of the good road: mindful of the word of St. Peter the apostle, saying: "Casting all your care upon Him: for He hath care of you."

ANOTHER

A certain brother when in trouble: had the habit of calling upon Jesus and His most loving Mother Mary. And when he was tempted by any bad passion or sadness; at once he had recourse to the Lord's Passion by the angel's prayer: calling upon Jesus and Mary to aid him against the temptation. One night therefore he saw in sleep the devil coming towards him: and intending to injure him. And as he feared to be hurt, and could not run away: he began silently to recite the Hail Mary. But when the other had heard Jesus named: at once he turned away from him, and commenced to flee and to run quickly. And seeing this: the brother cried still louder after him. Jesus, Jesus. And the louder he cried: the more quickly the devil ran, terrified by the sound of the sweet name of Jesus and of Mary His Mother. And suddenly falling he disappeared. Seeing this the brother awoke for joy of heart: and said: "If with one Hail Mary I can put the devil to flight: what have I now to fear."

ANOTHER

There was with us a certain laic named Egbert an old man and of advanced age: devout to God and the Blessed Virgin, and a fervent lover of holy poverty. He laboured hard according to his strength, digging the earth, and carrying it; and while sweating in toil, he used to think over the sorrows of the Lord's Passion: and when weary from labour for the relief of his body he gave himself to prayer. This man was long tempted by Satan to leave the monastery, and to go through the world begging: thinking that this would be more pleasing to God: and because he had many comforts here of which he was unworthy. But from this opinion he was withdrawn by the advice of the Prior and the warnings of the brothers, lest he should expose himself to danger: and wandering through the world finally go astray. For often the cunning tempter deceives the simple under the guise of a better good: and draws them from the good they have undertaken by change of place, to inconstancy of mind. And while he was still very little satisfied to remain: and yet did not dare to go away rashly without permission: amidst these temptations he had recourse to the Blessed Virgin through the devout advocacy of her prayers. One day then wearied from toil, he lay down to pray near his barrow: as he was very often wont to do, invoking Our Lady and calling on Jesus by name. While then he lay prostrate on the earth alone: he was lulled to sleep a little by a gentle sleep in the Lord. And he beheld a most venerable Lady standing by him: and saying these words in loving warning: "You should abide in this place: and what the Prior advises you and says, this do." And when she had spoken thus, the noble Lady at once disappeared: and he coming to himself and awakened wept most plentifully. Then he went in all haste to the Prior: and related to him in order with sobs and tears the things that he had seen and heard. To whom the Prior as a good shepherd consoling his sorrowful sheep replied: "This please me well, dear Egbert. Abide with us: as Our Lady has just showed and told you." Nor did he long survive after that; but persevering with much patience in obedience, to receive eternal rewards for short toil: with a good end he fell asleep in the Lord during matins on the octave of St. John apostle and evangelist. Anno Domini, 1420.

SERMON XXII

OF THE PRAISE OF THE MOST SWEET NAME OF JESUS: AND OF HIS MOST SWEET MOTHER MARY

BY spirit is sweet above honey: and my inheritance above honey and the honey-comb. Worthily, indeed, and very beautifully, brethren, the words of eternal wisdom are referred to the Mother of mercy of whom arose the sun of justice Christ. Sweet is Jesus, sweet Mary: and there is not in them any bitterness: but supreme gentleness, mildness, love, and mercy without measure. Blessed he who cleaves to the steps of the humble Jesus, and devoutly turns himself to His Mother: to find favour in their sight. Gather together then, most faithful servant of God, into one bundle the actions of Jesus, what He did and said: and they will profit thee more than all the treasures of the world. Go over also by thyself with earnest mind the acts and words of the most holy Mother of Jesus: and they shall be comforting to thy soul: and most sweet above all spices. The body receives pleasure from sweet odours, and is refreshed by the remedy of food: but the soul is nourished, strengthened and rejoiced by true virtues and holy meditations. But the more perfect studies one pursues, and the more noble masters one follows: the more clearly he learns: and the more speedily he arrives at the summit of blessedness. Sovereign masters of virtue, and lights of all holiness are Jesus and Mary; whom thou shouldst set before thee according to the measure of thy littleness: and look upon as if present. Join thyself to them: show thyself attentive and devout to them. Wherever thou hearest anything said concerning Jesus and Mary: there diligently lend thy ear: there tarry long: and weigh what edification and hidden sweetness there be within. As often also as thou comest to perform the Divine Work: or when thou art called to the common labour, or to some private task: first raise thy eyes to Heaven, and especially call upon Jesus and Mary: and suppliantly commend thyself to their constant protection. Offer thyself also to their good-pleasure in everything that is to be done; that thy action may be pleasing to God: profitable to the neighbour, and wholesome to thyself. Let thy intention be always pure: let thy goodwill be fervent: let thy work be discreet, thy speech circumspect: thy performance persevering, unto the praise of the holy name of Jesus, and the honour of His blessed Mother. Here commence to praise, venerate and love: that hereafter thou mayest merit to reign with them: and for ever with the holy angels to praise, bless and proclaim them. The praise of Jesus is sweet and beautiful: the praise of Mary lovable and bright. When joyous therefore praise, when sad pray: for they are worthy of all praise: and constantly to be invoked at all times. The more frequently thou exercisest thyself in their praise; the more shalt thou grow in their love: and the stronger thou shalt become in the grace of devotion. They will never be unmindful of thee: if thou art never unmindful of them. And if thou neglect them, which God forbid; or behave thyself ill, which may God keep far away: or grow lukewarm in the devotion which thou hast commenced, which may God not suffer: it will be needful to scourge thee with meet chastisement, and to bring thee back to right mind by adversity: that thou mayest learn to converse with God with greater care: and to guard grace bestowed with greater watchfulness for the future. And then be mindful of these benefactors: and bewail thy negligence and great ingratitude: which thou hast foolishly committed. Happy he who merits to hear the admonitions of Jesus in spirit, to amend himself unto better: that thereby after bitter tears, he may be again rapt into sweet ecstasies. For the loving kindness of Jesus surpasses all the sins of the world: and the indulgence of Mary can never be exhausted.

O if thou couldst make much progress in the love and praise of Jesus: and serve worthily and devoutly His blessed Mother Mary. But what wilt thou do since thou art not worthy to call them by name at all: seeing that thou art a man weak, lukewarm and careless, in many things also frequently offending? How then shalt thou praise: since praise is not seemly in the mouth of a sinner? For it is seemly that the holy should be praised by the just and worthy. Must thou keep silence then or say something? Woe to thee if thou dost not praise: and woe to thee if thou dost open unworthy lips. What shalt thou do to find mercy; and not to incur offence? Naught is better to obtain the goodwill of the most gentle Jesus and of the most pitiful Mary His Mother, than that thou humble thyself in all things: and bow thyself beneath all, and set thyself in the lowest place: truly entertaining unworthy and lowly sentiments of thyself: and bringing thyself back to nothing if thou hast felt anything good. Thus shall God be appeased: and Jesus shall have mercy on thee. Mary also shall pray for thee: and thou shalt be comforted in thy lowliness. Thou shalt not be ashamed from their face: but thou shalt receive plentifully rendering canticles of praise. And if thou canst not praise worthily, do what thou canst: give what thou hast. For the pious intention will refresh thee: until thou becomest more rich to render better service. Those who are great and very devout praise magnificently and devoutly: but those who have little oil: let them willingly offer even this to the Son of oil and the Mother of grace. It seems that one ought to be silent because of the surpassing glory and dignity of the glorious seed of the Virgin Mother: but since Mary does not spurn the little and sinners, she will mercifully admit thy shouting in the crowd of them that praise: as the holy Prophet says: "The poor and needy shall praise thy name." Therefore a little should be said to arouse devotion: and if not very elegantly: nevertheless of a more humble kind and more ready affection according to the measure of strength.

Who are the most sublime in Heaven; and the most lowly on earth? Are they not Jesus and Mary? Jesus made Himself a servant: Mary called herself a handmaid. The charity of both the whole world has experienced; their worth the citizens of Heaven proclaim: the host of angels worship. O if thou couldst be among them: and with untiring voice praise together the sweet name of Jesus and of the most sweet Virgin Mary. O how good and pleasant it is to serve these: who have served us both faithfully and humbly. Ye sons of men serve the Lord: Who has very often deigned to serve you. Serve ye the Mother of God: who has shown you an example of holy service. O how befitting it is to honour these sovereign patrons: Who can aid more than all others: through Whose hands the judgements of Heaven pass and are fulfilled. Every hour then we should beseech them, who protect us from the foes of body and mind: and bestow everlasting bliss upon their clients. In every need whatsoever have recourse to Jesus and Mary; unfold to them all thy burden: confess thy faults, bewail thy guilt. Seek forgiveness, seize hold of penance; take up hope again, promise amendment: and trust well in the help of grace. If thou fallest easily: take care to rise the more speedily. They willingly grant the prayers of the suppliant, they spurn not the groaning of the poor: yea even the holy angels shall rejoice over thee, when thou shalt be converted with thy whole heart from all deformity of sin: and shalt take up a better life according to the pattern of Christ, and of the Mother of blessed Jesus. Do thou be only on thy guard against offending: and they will not refuse the protection desired. Do thou show due reverence: and they will have a most sure care of thee. Amen.

A PRAYER

To Thee O Lord Jesus and to Thy most holy Mother the Virgin Mary: I entrust my soul and my body to be guarded unto life eternal. O my only hope Jesus and Mary: in every distress and anguish may your loving-kindness succour me. You are my most powerful Patrons: worthy of love above all the saints. I have not, poor as I am and a pilgrim in this world, friends so faithful and dear of all that are dear and known to me: as I trust in you.

SERMON XXIII

OF THE DEVOUT SERVICE OF THE BLESSED VIRGIN AND THE REMEMBRANCE OF HER NAME

BY memory is unto everlasting generations. Mary is the friend of poverty, the way of humility: the pattern of patience, and in all things perfect. From the beginning of the birth of Jesus she led a life of poverty: and unto its issue on the cross, she constantly held to patience. Let it please thee to follow her: to honour her with humble and devout service is befitting: and daily it behoves to weigh: what mark of thankfulness and special love should be most earnestly paid. Thou wouldst willingly rejoice with Mary in Heaven: bear also willingly poverty and contempt with Mary upon earth. Behold her humble ways, and her maidenly modesty amid her companions: and restrain thy levity, and shun tumult. Beware of displeasing Jesus and Mary by vain words: and unworthy actions. For it is not a light thing: to displease such dear Patrons. They see everything thou doest; and as thou showest thyself in amendment: so wilt thou experience them in thy aid. However their wisdom surpasses thy malice: and their indulgence brings thee to repentance. If thou dost recognize thy faults: change thy state unto a better. Persevere in good: and devoutly render thanks to God for His blessings. Thus did blessed Mary when she was filled with the Holy Ghost: and bare Jesus in her womb. Learn by the example of her mildness to bear piously the troubles that befall thee: and submit thyself to the divine ordinance, as it was ordained from eternity. Jesus will be thy helper; Mary will be to thee a faithful Mother: be thou a good son and a devout servant ready for ever good work.

Dost thou wish to do what is pleasing to the blessed Virgin?
Be humble, patient: sober, bashful, chaste.
Be fervent, mild: intern, of mind devout.
Go seldom forth: read, write, and often pray.

The service of Mary should not seem long, or burdensome. It is delightful and joyous: to serve such a Lady with heart and voice. For it shall not be without notable recompense: whatsoever little thing shall have been performed in her honour. The lowly Mother does not spurn little services; the loving Virgin willingly accepts small offerings: when they are offered freely and devoutly. She knows that we cannot give great things: nor does the pitiful Lady, the meek Queen demand impossibilities of her servants. That noble nature cannot refrain from pity for the needy: which brought forth mercy for the whole world. O how graciously she receives them that faithfully serve her: who has so frequently converted by her admonitions, and by evident miracles men who were living miserably in the world. How many would have been eternally damned, or would have bided obstinate in despair: if the most gentle Virgin Mary had not interceded for them with her Son. Meetly then is it said of her, that she is pitiful to all the wretched: and the help of all sinners. She does not seek, or need what we have: whose beck the heavens obey. She loves our good when she exacts service of us; she desires our salvation: when she requires that we pay her praise. And when she sees that the memory of her name is celebrated; thence she seeks an occasion to do us good: for she delights to repay her servants. She is most faithful to her promises: and most generous in her gifts. She is full of delights: and ever enjoys the harmony of the angels. Nevertheless she takes pleasure in the service of men: that the honour of God and the salvation of many may thence be more abundantly procured. She is moved by the tears of the wretched, she compassionates the sorrows of the distressed: she succours the perils of the tempted: she bows down to the prayers of the devout. If a man readily and humbly has recourse to her, and calls upon her sweet and glorious name: he shall not depart from her empty-handed. She has many who cleave to her; and the choirs of the angels obey her: and these she can send to the solace of the destitute. She commands the demons, that they presume not to trouble anyone: who submits himself to her dominion and charge. The evil spirits dread the Queen of Heaven: and they flee when they hear her holy name, as from fire. They fear the holy and terrible name of Mary: which to Christians is most lovable and ever glorious. They dare not appear and are unable to exercise their wiles: where they know that the name of Holy Mary shines forth. As if a thunderbolt had fallen from Heaven, they are overthrown at the sound of Holy Mary; and the more often it is uttered, and lovingly invoked: the more speedily and the further are they put to flight.

Again the holy angels and the spirits of the just rejoice, and are glad over the devotion of the faithful: that they so lovingly and earnestly celebrate the memory of Holy Mary: whose honourable name is shown forth in all the bounds of the churches: which have been especially dedicated to her name. And it is befitting and meet, that in preference to all the saints of God the Mother should be honoured by the dwellers of earth: whom the world of angels worships with highest praise. The name of Mary then is to be venerated by all the faithful, ever to be loved by the devout, embraced by religious, commended to the people, preached to sinners: suggested to the afflicted, invoked in all dangers. For she is the nearest to God and the most dear to the Son of God her Child the blessed Jesus; able faithfully to intercede for all the tearful sons of Adam: that He forgive their sins, and succour them in their perils. For when the occasion presents itself, she does not delay to whisper a good word in the ears of her Son: and to implore mercy for the needy. And she shall be most speedily heard in every cause entrusted to her, for her singular reverence: for her loving Son Jesus the Author of the salvation of the human race, honours her denying her nothing. Wherefore let all the faithful and devout desirous of escaping the shipwreck of the world, and of reaching the harbour of eternal salvation: fly to Our Lady St. Mary; whose unspeakable kindness tastes to the wretched most sweet, and cleaves to them most strongly: so that rightly may most abundant confidence be placed in her. Truly from infancy mercy grew up with her; nor hath it left her in Heaven that now she should be unmindful of her poor: but it has filled her most plentifully and sweetly. And although she be the highest of all, and encompassed with most blissful joys: nevertheless she is not forgetful of her lowliness: whereby she most worthily merited to be raised above all. And therefore does she know how to bow graciously to her least servants: rejoicing to become the advocate of the miserable: and to be called the mother of the orphaned. Amen.

SERMON XXIV

OF THE SORROW AND CONSOLATION OF THE BLESSED VIRGIN MARY

IYIELDED a sweet odour: like the best myrrh. The examples of the dear Virgin Mary: are to be recalled by thee with utmost love. For she as choice myrrh brought forth sweet-smelling fruit in patience: and was most pleasantly refreshed with most plentiful comfort of divine sweetness. A most mighty comfort thou also shalt find: if thou bearest the name of Mary grafted on thy heart. For thou shalt have many good things: if thou art well with Mary. The love of holy Mary drives out all heat of carnal concupiscence: and brings the refreshment of chastity. The love of holy Mary makes one despise the world: and serve Christ in humility. The love of holy Mary preserves from all evil companionship: and trains unto the purity of religious life. Love then holy Mary: and thou shalt obtain a special grace. Call upon Mary: and thou shalt gain the victory. Honour Mary: and thou shalt have an everlasting reward. Two benefits in particular are obtained: by the frequent bringing to mind of the holy life of Mary. In prosperity she teaches thee to praise God from thy inmost heart: and in adversity to keep thyself patient. She without interruption praised God most highly for blessings received: which she had received from Him in a manner more excellent than all others. She ever showed herself mild in the distresses of this world: and chose rather contempt than prosperity. She spent no day without grief: but yet she was not without great consolation amid her anguish. For every tribulation accepted for Christ brings sweetness and joy; and the more frequently a man is stricken by the blows of adversity: the more he merits to be enriched with mightier gifts. For the blessed Virgin grieved vehemently for the errors of the world and the malice of many: she compassionated the truly penitent and the hard tried. She grieved for the great ingratitude of men, to whom God the Father sent His only begotten Son made man for love: that they might return to the Paradise lost of old through Adam. She grieved for the loss of the wicked who refused to hear the word of God: who loved the world rather than Heaven: and sought after false riches rather than true virtues. She grieved for the oppression of the innocent and the violence of the evil: for the despising of the poor and the uplifting of the proud: for the negligence of divine worship, and the transgression of God's commandments. And because the whole world was seated in wickedness: and few disposed themselves to see the eternal light which had enlightened the world: the Mother of supreme love abounded in occasions of compassion. Herein she was most patient, leading a life full of martyrdom: pouring out tearful prayers with sobs for the salvation of souls. And if thou wilt consider further what and how much she endured in the persecution and Passion of her beloved Son; thou shalt find in sooth that she drank as many cups of bitterness in life: as Jesus had moments of age and wounded members. For when did Jesus suffer any desertion and rejection by men: and she did not faint away with compassion? If she sorrowed when she lost Jesus for an hour; how much did she weep when she saw Him crucified and die? It is known to the lovers of Jesus: for the affection of the Mother in compassion surpassed the usual measure of the devout. Therefore if thou desirest to feel the strength of the grief in the Mother: think of the vehemence of the love in the Virgin.

Again no one can express the joy of Mary: no one can grasp the abundance of her sweetness and the greatness of her consolation: for there is greater joy and consolation there: where there is wont to be a fuller infusion of grace and a more frequent visitation of God. Hence also ever arises a more ardent affection of divine praise: and the state of the whole interior man is renewed. Heavenly grace does not suffer a holy soul loving God above all to live without interior consolation: but it continually lifts her to things above, and wisely enlightens her in her actions; it enkindles her in holy meditations: and renders her devout in giving thanks. But the greater the grace, and the more stainless the life: the more joyous the conscience, and the more devout the prayer of praise. For this manner of life cut off from earthly tumult, and held back by no desires of things below, daily longs to be set in the heavenly choirs: is lifted above present things: and burns to enjoy the unceasing glory of the sovereign Trinity. Which glory no one of the saints tasted so purely in this life, as the blessed and glorious Virgin Mary: who became the most ardent in prayer of all them that contemplate and bless God.

Do thou also even now imitate the Mother of God, hearing the recital of her praises: that thou also mayest merit by the prayers of the Virgin Mother to be classed in the number of the devout. Strive earnestly to follow the most holy Mary in the aforesaid footsteps of virtue: unto the attaining of the palm of heavenly glory. Be much saddened also for thy past negligences, and the shortcomings not yet overcome: whereby thou hast offended God and all creatures. Thou didst act wickedly in the world: thou hast lived lukewarmly in the service of Christ; and therefore thou shouldst first mourn over thyself: then by charity over the neighbour. Pity therefore the danger of them that live ill: whom eternal punishment threatens, unless they repent of their sins. Many do ill and know it not: many more recognize their wickedness: and yet do not amend. For these must thou grieve and pray: that God may give them the spirit of compunction unto salvation. Pray also for friends and benefactors, for thy adversaries and detractors; that to the pious may be given worthy grace, to the hateful a good thought: and to all the peace of Christ with mercy. Pray that all may love God, and keep His commandments: that rational creatures may glorify their Creator: for whose sake God wrought all His wonderful works, and emptied Himself: humbly subject to Mary and Joseph. Again be thankful for the divine blessings most worthily vouchsafed to the whole human race through the most holy Mother of God: rendering her also reverence and honour. For since the law of nature bids us show always reverence and love to the parents of the flesh; much more should the children of the Church be thankful and devout to the Mother of grace: and love the Mother of God above all kinsfolk and acquaintance.

It behoves thee also to learn with Mary to rise to God with joyous praise; and faithfully to trust on her patronage, not to confide in thy own strength: that thy mind may not be kept back in things below weighed down by passions; but that daily enkindled with fresh desires it may freely rise upward: where with Jesus the King of angels the glorious Queen of Heaven, the pious Virgin Mary happily reigns. But alas, human weakness compels to come down afresh into this vale of tears: after a brief taste of divine consolations. And then again it is needful to cry to the Mother of many mercies; that she may whisper to her Son that thou hast no wine of fervour: but that thou dost need the sacred ointment of devotion, to praise Him with due reverence. For she has care of the poor and despisers of the world: and of the despised in the world for the sake of Jesus and the gospel of the kingdom. And therefore it is very profitable to know the place of refuge from the face of the enemy: where thou mayest be protected from the sharp arrows: where thou mayest lie hid from the cold and the storms of tribulation. There is no safer place to hide than the bosom of Mary: nor a horse more swift to escape the hand of the pursuer: than the prayer of faith sent into the castle of our royal Lady Saint Mary. For Jesus also Himself entered this castle: taking thence the sacred members of His body, to fight the prince of darkness. Do thou therefore also enter under the shelter of this fortress; praying day and night to be delivered from all threatening evils by the merits of the most holy Virgin: hiding securely under the most ample and most lovely mantle of Our Lady. For when holy Mary prays: the whole wicked crowd shall be put to flight. When Mary aids: thou shalt escape all dangers. There the poor man has his dwelling: there the sick finds a remedy: there the sad finds solace: there the troubled receives counsel: there the destitute obtains help. Well will it be with thee and very well: if thou prove thyself so worthy and obedient to the good pleasure of holy Mary; as to gain her favour now: and glory with all the elect hereafter. Hold her and do not let her go until she bless thee: and lead thee by a happy guidance to the palace of Heaven. Amen.

SERMON XXV

OF THE EXCELLENCE OF THE MERITS AND OF THE PRIVILEGES OF THE GIFTS OF THE BLESSED VIRGIN MARY

MANY daughters have gathered together riches: thou hast surpassed them all. Beloved brethren, be faithful servants of Jesus Christ: and devout lovers of His most holy Mother the Virgin Mary: if you desire to rejoice with them for ever in Heaven. Then shall you be dear to God and His blessed Mother: if you be humble of heart and chaste of body: if in all your manner of life modest, provident, God-fearing and prudent, you give no man occasion of scandal: or of just complaint. It is much for your salvation, for the honour of God, and the praise of the blessed Virgin, that you be devout in prayer; studious in reading, strenuous in toil, quiet in the dormitory: watchful in choir, cheerful in singing, amenable in Chapter, docile in receiving admonition: strict in silence, sober in refreshment, guarded in the eyes: and disciplined in all your ways. If therefore you desire worthily to praise the blessed Virgin, and supremely to venerate her: then be as simple children of God without malice, without guile: without wickedness, without lying; without anger, without quarrelling, without murmur, without suspicion: bearing all that is contrary to you in brotherly love, with humility and patience, for the sake of Jesus and Mary, and of imitating the life of the saints; for the sake of your own peace and the edification of others: and especially for the sake of enjoying the glory of the holy Trinity. For all bitter things become sweet: all burdens are lightened: when the love of Jesus and the memory of His loving Mother penetrate to the interior of the heart. If anyone desires to prove this: let him of them often think, speak, read, sing, and pray.

But that you may realize a little the most excellent worth of the most blessed Virgin Mary: hear a few of the many gifts and privileges, wherewith

God has blessed and exalted her above all the holy angels and archangels in Heaven: and above all men on earth. This is the most sacred Virgin and the most dear Mother of God: of whom in holy Church spread throughout the world we sing: "The holy Mother of God is exalted: to the heavenly kingdoms above the angel choirs." Recall therefore diligently the doings of old of the holy patriarchs: of whose stock sprang the Mother of God Mary as a rose without a thorn amid thorns. For as in former days by many holy men, patriarchs and prophets, by judges and kings, by priests and levites Christ the Son of God was foretold as one Who should be born of a Virgin for the redemption of the world, and suffer on a cross: so by divine ordinance very befittingly and wisely the most blessed and most devout Virgin Mary was foreshadowed and preconized by the holy maidens of that time, by illustrious women, by chaste widows, by devout prophetesses, and by the other religious women living in chastity: and for the protection of their modesty enclosed with their maids from the sight of men in their homes and chambers. She is in truth by the witness of the holy Scriptures the Virgin most prudent of all virgins, of all women the most bashful, of all maids the most beautiful, of all matrons the most venerable, of all ladies the most lovely, of all queens the Queen most noble; in whom all maidenly beauty, all moral virtue, all theological speculation, all loving devotion, all activity of virtue, all perfection of holiness, unite, indwell, and most abundantly shine forth: who has not, nor had, nor is to have, her like before her, or her equal after her. And as of old the material temple of Solomon was adorned above all the temples of the earth, and most widely renowned and most richly endowed, was honoured with magnificence by kings and peoples; so the spiritual temple of God, which is the blessed Virgin Mary, pure from every stain, shines above all the temples of the saints: and therefore should be more fully honoured and loved.

O truly renowned offspring nobly shooting forth from the glorious stock of the patriarchs: magnificently issuing from the priestly race: most worthily descended from the pontifical dignity: most truly foretold of the choir of prophets: most illustriously born of the royal family: most directly sprung from the lineage of David: most splendidly generated from the sublime tribe of Juda: most happily begotten of the people of Israel: singularly forechosen of the chosen people of God: most peacefully coming forth for the light of the world by divine pre-ordinance from parents holy and religious and pleasing to God. O happy and spotless Virgin Mary, most worthy of all praise and honour: to be embraced by all with all love and reverence. O glorious gem of virgins, thou from the beginning and before the ages wast pre-ordained by God, to bring forth the Redeemer of the world in the time decreed: desired by the patriarchs, foretold by the prophets: adopted by many kings and just; long awaited by the most devout people of Israel: and at length openly manifested to a sick world by God in His mercy. O sacred and most illustrious Virgin Mary: how noble and praiseworthy is thy name in the whole earth. For from the rising of the sun even to the going down in divers parts of the world, by Jews and Gentiles, by Greeks and Latins, by Romans and Germans, thy name has been proclaimed through the gospel of Jesus Christ thy Son; and still daily thy noble name is preached in all the churches of God, in chapels and cloisters, in fields and groves dedicated to God, by the little and the great, by priests and doctors, and by the preachers of different Orders: who all in unison desire to praise and expound thee. For even to the stars of Heaven to raise thee, and above the dignity of the angels to praise aloud thy holiness and beauty all the spirits of the just are eager and glad: and for greatness of love and sweetness of devotion singing, praying, meditating and celebrating thy holy solemnities they weary not: according to that word of Wisdom: "They that eat me, shall yet hunger: and they that drink me shall yet thirst." Praise and glory to the most high God: Who has rendered thee, O Mary, the greatest grace above all the daughters of men in the world; and now has set thy seat near the throne of thy Son in the heavenly kingdom, in a place most sublime, above all the choirs of angels and saints, most beautifully prepared for thee from eternity: and most happily to remain to thee for ever.

O supremely venerable Virgin Mary, Mother and Daughter of the eternal King: to be blessed by the mouth of all, to be reverenced with every honour: most white in virginity, most profound in humility, most fervent in charity, most mild in patience, most full in mercy; most devout in prayer, most pure in meditation, most sublime in contemplation: most sweet in compassion, most prudent in counsel, most mighty in aid. Thou art the court of God, the gate of Heaven, the garden of delights, the well-spring of graces; the glory of angels, the joy of men, the pattern of morals, the brightness of virtues, the light of life: the hope of the needy, the health of the sick, the mother of orphans. O Virgin of virgins, all sweet and beautiful: brilliant as a star, red as a rose: shining as a jewel: bright as the sun and the moon in Heaven and on earth. O meek Virgin, innocent as a lamb: simple as a dove; prudent as a noble lady: serving as a humble handmaid. O holy root, lofty cedar: fruitful vine, most sweet fig tree, most wide-spreading palm: in thee are found all good things: and by thee eternal rewards are given us. We should all fly to thee then as children to their mother's bosom, and as orphans to their father's home, as long as we live: that by thy glorious merits and prayers we may be defended from all evils.

But now listen to the words of a certain doctor, concerning the twelve stars in the crown of the blessed Virgin: wherewith Our Lady St. Mary is resplendent above all the saints in Heaven. "These twelve stars are the twelve prerogatives of her brightness in reigning: which she has with respect to all other citizens above. For with regard to the Church militant: she has four special most brilliant gifts full of the works of mercy. For beyond all the others she listens more kindly, condescends more humbly; acts with more power, succours with greater frequency: as experience teaches in the difficult affairs of the Church. So also with regard to the Church triumphant: she has these four eminent prerogatives. For above all the others she is set higher in Heaven, she shines with greater brilliancy: she is loved more fervently, she is honoured more fully: as it is meet to think of her glorious merits. Again with respect to the holy Trinity, which beatifies: she has likewise four prerogatives or stars brighter than all constellations. For beyond all the others who contemplate the glory of the eternal Trinity, she beholds the holy Trinity itself more clearly: she is drawn to It more joyously, she contemplates It more intimately; and above all in Heaven she enjoys It more happily: of which things no one should longer doubt."

But hear further what of those stars saith blessed Bernard, the special lover of the blessed Virgin, the sweet doctor and devout instructor of monks. "On her head," he says, "a crown of twelve stars. Who shall value these gems? Who shall number the stars: of which the royal crown of Mary is composed? It is beyond man to expound the manner of this crown: to show its formation. We however, in the measure of our littleness, abstaining from the dangerous scrutiny of mysteries: may perchance not unseemingly understand these twelve stars as the twelve prerogatives of stars, wherewith Mary is singularly adorned. For we find in Mary the prerogative of Heaven: the prerogative of the flesh, and the prerogative of the heart. And if this number three be multiplied by four: we have haply twelve stars, wherewith the diadem of our Queen shines above all. For the first brightness flashes upon me in the generation of Mary: the second in the greeting of the angel: the third in the coming upon her of the Holy Ghost: the fourth in the ineffable conception of the Son of God." I leave it to your diligence to examine each single point more attentively: but for me let it be enough of many words to have quoted to you a few. If anyone wishes to know more fully the mystic sense of the stars: let him read that sermon of blessed Bernard, beginning with the theme: "A sign appeared in the Heaven," etc.

These things therefore, beloved brethren, for singular reverence and love of the most blessed Virgin Mary often revolve, ruminate with the mouth: and for giving of thanks most joyously sing the hymns and canticles of joy on her feasts and commemoration throughout the year. But especially before the altar of God and in presence of the image of the blessed Virgin bare your heads and bow: humbly bend the knee, as if you saw Mary present in the body speaking with the angel, or holding her Son in her bosom: and then lifting up your eyes with good hope of the salvation for which we look, most lovingly implore the help of mercy from the Mother of mercy, and say: "O most merciful Mother of God Virgin Mary, Queen of Heaven, Mistress of the world, joy of the saints, solace of sinners, heed the groans of the contrite, fulfil the desires of the devout: succour the necessities of the weak, comfort the hearts of the distressed: assist the agonizing, protect thy suppliant servants from the harassing of the demons: bring thy lovers with thee to the reward of everlasting blessedness: where with thy most loving Son Jesus Christ thou reignest most happily for ever. Amen."

SERMON XXVI

ON THE FEAST OF ST. AGNES, VIRGIN AND MARTYR

OF THE THREE LOVELY GARMENTS OF MOST BLESSED AGNES, VIRGIN

THE Lord hath clothed me with the garment of salvation: and with the robe of gladness He hath encompassed me. Beloved brethren, these words are recited and sung of the holy virgin Agnes, the noble spouse of Christ and our glorious patroness: whose festal day in the yearly cycle we must solemnly celebrate: and implore her glorious suffrages with devout prayer. And may she deign to pray for us all, who is greatly loved by Our Lord Jesus Christ; and most favourably regarded in His eyes and by His most sacred Mother Mary: when she petitions for any pious cause. O may she not forget now to pour forth her prayers so devout and acceptable to God in the heavenly kingdom; as formerly she wept and prayed for the Prefect's son who had perished miserably: whom she raised from the dead by the gift of the grace of Christ. Mark therefore the words quoted above in the beginning of this sermon: as if you now heard them with your own ears from the mouth of the most blissful Agnes. Consider the loveliness of the garments of the most noble virgin: wherewith Jesus Christ her heavenly Spouse clothed and adorned her within rather than without. For she was worthy to be clothed by Christ with the garment of salvation, and to be decked with the robe of gladness: who spurned all worldly adornment, and for the love of her immortal Spouse shed her blood: and cheerfully accepted precious death for eternal life. There she now rejoices with her most loving Spouse and the holy angels, with the most glorious Mother of Jesus and numberless bands of maidens, set in the higher choirs of the virgins; following the Lamb whithersoever He goeth, and singing the sweet canticles of joy given to virgins only to sing: which surpass the music of all organs and the melody of all minstrelsy. Moreover she merited to have this prerogative on earth: that the memory of her most blissful name should be venerated with never-ending praise in the Church, and most devoutly celebrated: and should be magnificently honoured by all the faithful of Christ. For truly great and holy doctors often commend, eminently praise, openly preach; and relate as an example to us all of lovable chastity the story of her passion and exhort with sublime encomium noble youths and maidens to love Christ.

But let us see now the lovely garments of holy Agnes: wherewith she is resplendent above all the raiment cunningly wrought by man. For very precious and beautiful are the robes, wherewith the souls of the saints are decked interiorly: which Christ brought to the world from the treasury of Heaven: when born of the Virgin Mary of a royal race for our salvation. Now there are in particular three kinds of garments, woven by the skill of the Holy Ghost: which Christ gave to St. Agnes His spouse as a present: so that she might love no other wooer but Himself alone: nor look upon, nor admit to her speech: lest haply he should lessen, or darken, or extinguish her love: which would be most unbecoming, and would especially hinder the devoutness of her prayer.

The first garment then wherewith most blessed Agnes, one of the wise virgins, was clothed is a long white robe: brighter than glass, more spotless than fine linen, whiter than the snow. And this is called inviolable virginity: dear to God, agreeable to the angels: most venerable to men. This holy garment, pleasing to God, from her childish years, yea from the very cradle did the most chaste Agnes put on, and preserve unspotted: who in the very beginning of creeping babyhood was offered by her parents to God, and espoused to Christ with the ring of faith: so that she could never be torn from the love and espousals of her heavenly Bridegroom by any reasoning, or power, or threats or flattery: but she remained a virgin for ever: and for faith and chastity hesitated not to die. This garment has at the bottom a golden hem cunningly worked by the finger of God: whereon are contained the honied names Jesus and Mary, as also the noble names of all the other holy virgins, befittingly inscribed in alphabetical order; examples to follow the blessed footsteps of Jesus Christ, and of His blessed Mother the ever Virgin Mary: for the blissful obtaining of heavenly glory.

The second garment is red or purple, coloured with the precious blood of the Lamb without spot Jesus Christ: and brightly adorned with numerous white flowers. And this is called unconquerable patience: or unwearying constancy. On this robe are found all the symbols of the Lord's Passion, and the holy stigmata: which also are seen imprinted on the loving soul by the goad of interior sorrow at the four corners, before and behind. Now these are signs of divine love: and a shield of invincible patience against the shafts of the devil: namely, the holy cross, the nails, the lance, the rod, the cord, the pillar: the white robe and the purple: the gall, the reed, the spittal, the scourges, the thorny crown: and the other many insults and cruel wounds. This garment also has a hem of silver, deep and broad: that is, a faith right, enlightened and strong unto death: whereon are discovered written in the colour of the rose the names of all the blessed martyrs, in Greek, Latin and Hebrew characters, according to the alphabetical order; which when diligently examined and read: encourages the distressed and tempted soul unto bearing all the adversities of this world. With this noble and purple robe was clad Our Lord Jesus Christ the King of Martyrs and the Spouse of Virgins in His happy and blessed Passion, bearing the crown of thorns and the purple garment for our salvation: to strengthen the hearts of the weak in their tribulation for whatsoever insult or wrong done them: that after short and passing distress in the world: they may merit to receive an unperishable crown in Heaven. For every tribulation patiently borne for Christ: brings a certain hope of reigning for ever with Christ. This holy and royal robe Christ gave His beloved bride, the noble maiden St. Agnes, at the time of the persecution of the Christians in the holy Roman city: that she might follow the footsteps of His sacred Passion; bear the insults and threats of the wicked with great constancy for the faith and for chastity: after the example of many martyrs and innumerable maidens, slain without cause for the name of Christ. For whose praise-worthy triumph and unspeakable glory: holy Mother Church now praises Christ and rejoices magnificently throughout the whole world. Happy the soul which struggles manfully against inrushing vices: and often sighs, and prays amid divers perils and burdens: to be speedily delivered from all stress and misery.

The third garment of St. Agnes is a golden mantle made of silk throughout as a veil of virginity: which encompasses, covers and decks the whole body of the virgin. And that it may shine the more brightly and please the beholders, it is interwoven and ornamented with many brilliant pearls, with many precious stones and sparkling gems. And this more noble than the other robes is woven by the skill of the Holy Ghost; and it is called fitly and justly by the men of learning and understanding undying charity: of which it is said by blessed Paul: "Charity never falleth away: whether prophecies shall be made void, or tongues shall cease: or knowledge shall be destroyed." With this robe was clad most blessed Agnes: when questioned of her Spouse, as to who He was, she faithfully replied: "I love Jesus Christ, Whose chamber I have entered: Whose Mother is a Virgin: Whose Father knoweth not woman. Whom when I love I am chaste, when I touch I am pure: when I receive I am a maiden." This charity is supremely necessary for the adornment of the robe of virginity: for without charity virginity cannot please God: neither also shall the proud virgin be numbered among the wise virgins: who has not the oil of charity and of fervent devotion in the lamp of her heart. That therefore the virginal robe may shine brightly in the sight of God and the angels: the lover of chastity must guard herself from all pride of mind, and dissoluteness of mouth: lest haply deceived by negligence of interior things and concupiscence of the eyes for exterior things, she very much displease the eyes of the heavenly Bridegroom. Therefore let her hold all her senses and words in every place and at all times strictly under religious discipline: and attribute the whole good of chastity faithfully and entirely to God: Who has deigned to bestow upon her so chosen a gift unto the beauty of her soul. Moreover with great humility and daily supplication let her longingly seek from Christ: that she may constantly persevere even unto the end chaste, sober and modest, as becomes a virgin of Christ; and that she may be able to overcome all the lusts of the flesh, and cast away all worldly cares, as long as she subsists in this frail body: for she lives in the midst of foes and many perils. This charity is also very needful for the adornment of the second virginal robe, which is called unconquerable patience: for patience without the charity of Christ does not profit unto salvation and the merit of life eternal: even if a man bear the tearing of wild beasts, or fire, or sword, or the torment of the cross. For suffering does not make the martyr: but the good cause makes the holy martyr; who suffers for the faith of Christ, or for justice, or for chastity: and especially for the salvation of souls. Now Christ bestowed these three precious garments upon most blessed Agnes in sign of His exceeding love and perpetual espousals; which she very gratefully received: and with great joy adorning herself within said: "The Lord hath clothed me with the garment of salvation: and with the robe of gladness He hath encompassed me." And again: "The Lord hath clad me with a mantle wrought in gold: and with large jewels He hath decked me." Clothed then from Heaven in these sacred garments, and protected as by a triple buckler: the most blessed maiden the youthful Agnes went forth, to fight against the three battalions of the devil; to wit, against the delights of the flesh, the riches of the world: and against the threats of wicked men. Thanks be to Almighty God, our most mighty helper, the King invisible, and the immortal Spouse, the Creator of all things; Who strengthened the heart of the maiden that she might conquer: guarded untouched the body of His bride; preserved unharmed the innocent lamb amid the flames: and so strongly enkindled her heart unto the love of His most holy and honied name: that she chose rather to die, than break troth with her heavenly Spouse: Whom she had vowed herself to serve by an everlasting bond. O truly admirable constancy of the maiden: O how praiseworthy the patience of holy Agnes: who amid such great temptations and persecutions, amid so many clamours, derisions, flatteries, terrors, and armed men brandishing their swords, held to the purpose of virginity; and feared not to acknowledge openly before her foes that Christ was her Bridegroom: but with great constancy describing in terms of praise many wondrous things of the nobility, of the beauty and power of Christ her Spouse, cried saying: "I am espoused to Him, Whom angels serve: at Whose beauty the sun and the moon marvel. To Him alone I keep troth: to Him with utter devotion I commit myself." And rightly, indeed. For He alone is the true God, mighty in Heaven and on earth: seated above the cherubim and seraphim He beholds the abysses and the secrets of the heart. He regards the humble: and the proud He knows only afar off. He does not accept the person of man: but in all keeps a right judgement: giving to each truly that which is due. He knows all things from eternity: and with supreme providence He rules all things. He tries His elect in many ways, and rewards them richly for much patience in Heaven; but the wicked on account of their malice He severely punishes and condemns: preserving in all this great mercy with full justice. To Whom be everlasting praise and glory: for unending ages of ages. Amen.

SERMON XXVII

OF THE GOLDEN CROWN ON THE HEAD OF MOST HOLY AGNES, VIRGIN

AND as a bride: He hath decked me with a crown. Beloved brethren, now hear a little, if it please you, concerning the crown of the most holy virgin Agnes, wherewith Christ crowned her in Heaven. The crown is an ornament of the head and a sign of very great dignity: which is due especially to kings and to the sons and daughters of kings because of the nobility of their birth; or also to certain great personages in token of victory, or learning, or holiness: or exceeding virtue. Whence of the holy martyrs in particular we read and sing: "A crown of gold upon his head: set as a sign of holiness." But who shall worthily describe the beauty of this crown? Methinks that no mortal man can know it, unless he to whom God reveals this mystery: or he who by His grace attains the kingdom of God after death. This golden crown surpasses all the glory of this world and the splendour of both kings and princes, and the mitres of both nobles and prelates; for it is not wrought of earthly material: but prepared in the heavenly workshop by God, it shines with ever fresh brightness. And what better and more worthy for our fancy can we understand by this crown; than Our Lord Jesus Christ Himself the giver of eternal glory? For He is the essential reward and crown of all the saints: the beginning and end of all good things. He is supreme happiness, supreme bliss: supreme beauty, sovereign sweetness. He is eternal truth, eternal wisdom: eternal goodness, eternal majesty. He is the most pleasant source of life; Who by His presence rejoices and inebriates all the citizens of Heaven: in mercy saves and crowns; by grace justifies and enlightens: by glory beatifies and satisfies. He draws all things to Himself, fills all things by Himself, exalts above all, and most superabundantly recompenses; giving to each a golden penny for his few labours: and for a brief struggle a golden crown to be possessed most fully with the angels in life eternal. To have this crown we ought all to toil and strive to overcome: as all the saints before us have done and have overcome; who now reign with Christ: and bear on their heads crowns of triumph for the hard labour of the conflict. Who however do not attribute to themselves the victory over the enemy; but with all reverence and gratitude lay down their crowns before the throne of God in the presence of the Lamb: and with boundless exultation and harmonious voice chant and say: "Blessing, brightness, wisdom, praise, honour, glory, salvation, virtue, victory to our God for ever: Who hath led us through many tribulations to the happy obtaining of this glorious crown." This golden crown with its aureole most blessed Agnes merited to receive abiding firm and constant in her passion for faith and chastity; giving herself up to death: that she might receive a crown of glory, never to be forfeited. What more lovely than this crown, what more pleasant, what more sublime, what more blissful; than most clearly to contemplate the King of angels with all the saints in Heaven?

O virgin of Christ despiser of the world, who hast chosen to serve Christ in chastity: rejoice in the hope of the glory to come. If thou desirest to wear a golden crown in Heaven; bear now Christ always in thy heart: always in thy mouth, always in thy work. Turn thine eyes away from the world: lift up thy soul to Jesus in Heaven. Be fervent in His praise, humble and vile in thine own eyes; frequent in prayer, ready in service, prudent in word: patient in pain, silent in reproaches, cheerful in contempt; simple in raiment, modest in manners: guarded in all thy ways. Do not neglect Christ in any work or moment of time under Heaven: Who never turns His eyes away from thee in whatsoever place thou mayest be. Look upon St. Agnes as if dwelling in the body: and showing thee an example of chastity. So holy, so chaste, so devout, so modest, so dignified, so guarded was most blessed Agnes in this life: that she did not lift her eyes to the idols of the gentiles, or to the spectacle of their games: or to the glittering of gold or silver: nor did she covet the beauty or the friendship of any mortal man; but bearing God in her mind, holding Him by faith, loving Him with her heart, praising Him with her mouth: with the whole desire of her soul she raised her eyes constantly to Heaven; where she knew was Christ her Spouse, the best treasure of her heart: One to be loved and embraced above all things desirable.

Therefore in order to excite still greater devotion, let us take pleasure in contemplating the beauty of the crown of most blessed Agnes: which decked with lovely flowers affords wondrous delight to chaste minds. For it has three silver circlets in honour of the holy Trinity: containing three garlands woven of flowers of most beautiful colour and sweetest odour. He who has ears to hear: let him hear and understand what these things mystically signify. Maidens rejoice in lovely dresses and flowers; soldiers in golden armour and shields: clerics in books and studies, monks in hymns and psalms; seculars in worldly things, princes in luxuries: spiritual men in things divine. But no delight is greater and sweeter: than to exult in God and in works of true virtue wrought to the honour of God. Leaving aside then things dangerous and perishable: with the chaste and sacred virgins let us examine with our inner eyes the unfading flowers in the crown of most blissful Agnes.

The first circlet contains a garland of white flowers and pure lilies: begotten and born in the valley of humility. These flowers designate holy and devout meditations on the Incarnation of Jesus Christ born of the pure and holy Virgin Mary; wrapped in clean swaddling clothes, placed in a narrow manger, suckled at her virginal breasts: honoured by angelic praises, visited by devout shepherds; made known by a brilliant star, sought, found and worshipped by holy kings: worthily venerated by the same with three gifts, the presentation of gold, incense and myrrh; embraced by holy Simeon in loving arms: by the widow Anna with heart and mouth supremely blessed and praised. In all these good things heard, read and meditated what else is found: but a garden full of flowers and lilies with many sweet herbs? Truly all these shine, flower, glow: are brilliant, sweet smelling and delightful. These flowers of the nativity of Christ and the ever virginity of blessed Mary His Mother have so sweet an odour, so wondrous a taste: so great a beauty, so strong a heat, that they drive all temptation and carnal love from the languid soul; all anger and wrath, all envy and pride: all sloth and luke-warmness, all hardness and trouble; all sadness and distrust, all wickedness and deceit: all turpitude and diabolical suggestion; whether from man or woman, whether from youth or ancient, whether from rich or poor: because for all was Christ born, for all He suffered and was crucified; that He might save all, cleanse all from sins: and deck them with the flowers of virtues.

And in this garland there are five lilies very necessary to virgins for the safeguard of chastity: to wit, modesty, silence, sobriety, solitude and the cloister. These strongly guard the virgin's court: and render her crown more bright. Listen O virgin to a virgin: commending holiness. "The virgin," he saith, "thinketh on the things that are the Lord's that she may be holy in body and in spirit in Christ Jesus Our Lord." Who is this Jesus, Whom holy virgins so love: as to leave even their parents? This is Jesus of Nazareth, the only-begotten of God the Father, the Son of the Virgin Mary, the Spouse of Agnes: the lover of chastity, the guardian of virginity. He is the comforter of the poor: the protector of widows, the receiver of orphans: Who speaks to virgins in the Canticle of canticles. "I am the flower of the field and the lily of the valleys: I am the visitor and indweller of holy minds." Wherefore, virgin of Christ, if thou wilt worthily please the heavenly Bridegroom: strive to have within virginal flowers and pure lilies: and to guard all thy senses from deceptions without. Beware of the hawk, O simple dove: flee the wolf, meek little lamb: beware of the serpent approaching thee, chaste maiden: lest by the windows of the body he enter the chamber of the heart: and the purity of thy conscience be corrupted by heedless sight or evil hearing: or by thy other senses always prone to evil. Therefore the greatest care must be taken with regard to places, persons, times, conversations, greetings, gifts: laughter, joking, sight, adornment, banquets, vain songs.

These and many other blandishments has the world: which alas it offers its lovers who run with blinded mind to the torments of hell. O foolish joys of the world: after which follow eternal lamentations. For all things beautiful and pleasant shall perish without delay: when the hour of death shall have come.

But these earthly and carnal delights are poisonous to virgins: they are to be dreaded by the modest, shunned by the devout: hated by religious, very greatly feared by the young: severely chastised in the older and the careless. For the true disciple of Christ and lover of chastity hides herself from the sight of men lest she displease God: lest she lose the comfort of the Holy Ghost lest haply it prove a danger and a stumbling-block to herself and others: and she become the laughing stock of the devil, who was the companion of angels. Therefore the more closely confined she remain in watchfulness and the discipline of the Order: the more beautiful lilies shall she have in her halo and golden crown. And when the virgin recluse, intending and desiring to please God alone, has removed and cleansed herself from all worldly cares and gossip: then by the breathing of the grace of Christ the sweet odour of a good life as the odour of myrrh and incense shall be shed from her: and many daughters of Sion still given to the world, hearing of the holy life of the enclosed nun, will be encouraged also to leave all the vanity of the world for the sake of Christ: to attain with the virgins the beauty of the golden crown. O how wisely dost thou act, daughter of Sion: who spurnest the perilous world; resolvest to espouse and ever to cleave to the King of angels: and hastenest to enter to the heavenly nuptials. Enter, enter the cloister of virgins, where thou mayest learn to do the will of the Lord thy King: and make ready thy heart watching with thy companions, praying and awaiting the blessed coming of thy Bridegroom from Heaven. Assuredly if thou dost persevere in what thou hast begun: it shall be without doubt as thou hast often longingly besought of the Lord thy God.

The second circlet of this golden crown contains a garland woven of red flowers, beautiful to see, delicious of odour, wondrous to hear, comforting to the heart. These roses designate chastisement of the flesh, contempt of the world, compunction of heart: and holy meditation with affection of intimate compassion towards the Passion of Our Lord. These roses grow amid thorns and briars and nettles: that is, amid divers temptations of the flesh and vexations of men; who disturb others now by harsh words, now by evil conduct: and often trouble the devotion of the peaceable man. Woe to them: and well is it for those who suffer annoyance from the perverse. These roses therefore are called red or purple: because they bring pain and blushing to bashful minds. Nevertheless they give forth a sweet fragrance, if they are roughly bruised: because humble minds answer sweetly and lovingly, when they are reproved and despised by the passionate: and they render the greatest thanks to God: that they have deserved to be wounded and pricked by the thorns of their neighbours. These roses set over the fire and burnt, give forth a sweet water profitable for medicine; likewise the mild and humble enkindled by the fire of the Holy Ghost piously intercede for the injurious and the envious: and often pour forth tears with groaning. Truly great are the merits of the patient, great the trophies of virgins; great with God and illustrious are the honours of the continent: to whom an eternal reward with a crown of gold, more brilliant than all the stars, shall be rendered in Heaven. O virgin meek and humble: very much canst thou merit in distresses borne for the name of Christ. For as often as thou dost patiently endure a harsh word or injurious action; so often dost thou beget and bring forth red roses from thorns: and addest fresh lustre to thy crown. These roses are found in great plenty among the holy martyrs and the virgins dedicated to God; who armed with faith, enflamed with love, and girdled with patience, shed abundantly for Christ their rose-red blood: and rejoicing in sovereign glory have merited to receive eternal triumphal crowns, brilliant with roses and lilies. Whence we read of St.Tiburtius a noble martyr of Christ; that commanded to walk barefoot upon live coal: he trusting in the Lord Jesus approached without fear: and making the sign of the cross stood upon the glowing embers unharmed: and with joyous soul replied to the judge: "In the name of Our Lord Jesus Christ, I seem to be walking upon rose blossoms: for the creature itself obeys the command of the Creator." Hence also of St. Dorothy a noble virgin and martyr it is most beautifully related: that praying a while before the hour of her passion she merited to receive from the Paradise of her heavenly Spouse Jesus Christ three most lovely roses with three sweet smelling apples: which by a child of angelic beauty she graciously sent to Theophilus a philosopher who had mocked her and an unbeliever. And when he saw them, he was converted and became a believer; and burning with the heat of faith, speedily following Dorothy by the palm of martyrdom, he joyously entered Paradise: as the beautiful bride of Christ Dorothy had promised him.

Let no one then despair of gaining those blushing roses: as if they were set afar off and were difficult to find. For they can be diligently sought and profitably found by all Christians and especially by religious and devout persons both day and night, both winter and summer: but they must be kept with care. For in reading the Passion of Christ and the sufferings of the holy martyrs, red roses are sought in the Church books: in meditation and prayer they are found: by living justly, soberly, chastely and piously they are gathered and preserved. And these red roses are to be sought more in time of trouble near the mount of Olives in a garden apart from the crowd: which Jesus and His disciples entered to pray. Who then taken by the Jews, bound, buffeted, scourged, crowned, crucified, wounded, and bleeding as it were from all His body: appeared more ruddy than any rose, dyed and empurpled with the red of His own precious blood. O how many red roses did the most meek Jesus bring forth from each of His bruises and wounds; sweeter and more lovely than all spices. For the more often these roses are beheld, the more roughly they are bruised, the longer they are revolved in the mind: the more mightily they give forth odour, sweeten, flower, redden, grow and dilate. For the roses of Jesus Christ of Nazareth, brought forth in the rosary of His Passion and crushed by the Jews in Jerusalem as in a mortar, surpass the sufferings of all the holy martyrs and virgins: in worth, greatness, sweetness, beauty, and fullness of all graces, from the rising of the sun, even to the bounds of the whole world. And these roses are very precious and suitable and lovely to deck the crown of every devout soul; so that they cannot be valued at any worldly price, or bought of merchants: or found in the stores of physicians. Where then can they be seen and obtained? Not in the market, but in the choir: not in the square, but in the Church: not in warfare, but in the cell: not in tumult, but in silence: not in laughter, but in mourning: not in feasting, but in fast. However they are found especially by despisers of the world who daily take up their cross, and very soon by those who seriously meditate upon the Passion of Christ: and they are very plentifully gathered during Mass. For they mightily refresh sorrowful souls: and comfort those that are cast down by adversity. But it behoves the devout soul to have a great watchfulness over herself: lest the cunning thief the devil come of a sudden into this garden of roses with his most wicked lies: and if he find the casket of the heart open, take thence the sweet roses of Christ: and silently cast in instead fetid nettles and black coals. Where is Jesus now, where the cross, where the nails, where the lance: to drive the malignant foe from thy casket? Arise and watch: cry and pray: call upon Jesus, worship the Crucified.

Mark thee with the sign of the holy cross against the foe of all virtue: seize the spear of the soldier Longinus against the terror of the raging lion: shut thy heart against the poison of the serpent: strengthen it with the three nails of the Lord as with three strong bolts: that so easy an entry to the secret of thy heart may not lie open to the cunning and rabid enemy.

The third circlet contains a garland woven most beautifully of blue and emerald flowers: sweet-smelling above all the herbs of the field, full of heavenly mysteries. For rightly do these flowers pertain to the beauty of the virginal crown: which keep purity with virgins. And if they are well understood: they aid not a little the virtues of religious: who have utterly forsaken earthly things. Therefore the blue flowers which have the appearance of the colour of the sky, designate the contemplation of heavenly glory and the great desire of the perfect and recluses: who forgetting all lower and perishable present goods, meditate the eternal: and ceaselessly pant for the presence of God and the fellowship of the angels: where all things are quiet, pleasant, and perfect. These often enkindled in prayer desire with blessed Paul to be loosed of the bond of the body; and with Elias to be carried to Heaven in a fiery chariot: and happily to be presented to Christ in His Kingdom; where they may ever rejoice and feast in the sight of God: praising and singing with the holy angels without any hindrance or fatigue the sublime praises of the sovereign Trinity unto everlasting eternities. These flowers, to wit, meditations of heavenly joys, greatly adorn the crown of every sacred virgin and faithful soul heartily loving Christ: and eagerly thirsting for God the living fountain. These sacred flowers are chiefly found and read in the gospel meadows and gardens of the Saviour: in meditation on the joys of the Lord's resurrection, and ascension, and the coming down of the Holy Ghost: and on the miracles gloriously wrought by the apostles of Christ in the primitive Church in the name of Jesus. In like manner from a special devotion flowers of heavenly gladness are gathered on the various feasts of the most blessed Virgin Mary, and on the festivals of other saints: when there is concerning them in the Church devout singing, reading, and celebration: and longing thought on the eternal glory of the saints. For so often do flowers of heavenly brightness arise, grow, and sweeten in the contemplative soul suspended in God: as often as the mind is touched and enkindled by the memory of heavenly glory: and sighs and pants for the presence of Christ and the saints. Whence often from fervent desires it looks upward: and from the inmost heart cries out with Elias and prays: "It is enough for me, O Lord, take away my soul: for better is one day in Thy courts above thousands of the joys of this life." But again it is to be considered that these noble roses then fall from the crown of the devout soul, are soiled and wither: when the mind commences to take pleasure in vain and curious things below, or is frivolously occupied without: and weighed down by a certain sloth, neglects to meditate on heavenly things which are ever preferable to visible: and better than all the treasures of the world. Whence also blessed Paul encouraging his disciples on to the flower-bearing fatherland says: "Seek the things that are above where Christ is sitting at the right hand of God: mind the things that are above not the things that are upon the earth." Why? Because the fashion of this world speedily passeth away: and nothing lasts under the sun that can satisfy the heart of man.

There are also in the virginal garland many very beautiful flowers of a yellow and a dark blue colour having the glow of fire: agreeable to the sight, sweet to the odour: soft and yielding to the touch. These belong to the active life: and signify the compassionate affections of the heart for the succour of the weak and sickly; and the sweet discourses from the mouth of the prudent man to console the sad and burdened: lest they faint in their temptations and daily toils. For thus the law of God prescribes and brotherly love demands: that the strong carry the weak, the prudent instruct the ignorant: the mild restrain the passionate, the fervent arouse the lukewarm: the joyous comfort the sad, the grave reprove the dissolute: the discreet restrain the over-eager, the humble repress the proud: the simple keep in the curious, the constant keep back the frivolous; the silent reprove the talkative: that he may rather edify his hearers by his silence than by a flow of words. From these yellow flowers a most sweet odour often breathes; which strengthens weak souls with spiritual remedies: that they may make greater progress in virtue. Hence it is that St. Paul adorned with many flowers of virtue: exhorts his disciples to gather the flowers of charity, saying: "By charity serve one another, for we are members of one another." And again, "Bear ye one another's burdens: and so you shall fulfill the law of Christ." These flowers of brotherly compassion and instruction are found most fully in the field of Our Lord's preaching: to wit, in the sweet sermons of Christ and in the eight beatitudes; in the mystic parables, and the happy revelations of the heavenly kingdom: in various signs on the sick and the possessed: in pity for the needy and poor; in kindness for sinners and the penitent: in meek words to the hard and perverse; in blameless life and humble service and want with His disciples: in weariness of His tender body, and long nights passed in devout prayer: on high mountains and retired places: suitable for meditating on heavenly joys. Behold as many as were His sacred discourses so many beautiful flowers: as many as His mystic parables, so many splendid roses. And when Jesus spoke to the apostles of the kingdom of God and the angels: then He showed His friends ethereal flowers in heavenly secrets. And when He gave them a new commandment that they should love one another; and washed their feet instructing them by word and example: then He shed among them a fragrance of most excellent odour from the yellow flowers.

O what a stupendous sign Jesus wrought: when He showed Himself to all as an example of true humility. O wonder above all wonders; that the most holy of all the saints and the most high of all lords should become the lowest servant of all His servants: that the sovereign majesty freely lowered itself below simple and poor men, His guests, saying: "I am in the midst of you as he that serveth: for I came not to be ministered unto: but to minister. If I being your Lord and Master have washed your feet: you also ought to wash one another's feet." What more, Lord? One ought to pray for another: to teach by example, to injure no man: to wish to do good to all. These flowers of brotherly compassion and pious assistance greatly adorn the crown of virginal purity and the life of religious observance: both in the contemplation of heavenly secrets and in the visiting of a sick neighbour. For then the flowers of virtue shed a sweeter perfume among brethren, and grow more luxuriantly, when the devout contemplator abandons the angelic ranks for a while: and joyfully goes to serve the sick and needy, as if he saw Christ in person. For when the studious reader of the Scriptures, or the diligent writer of books being called closes the volume and puts down the pen from his hand: and at the sound of the bell at once arises and goes to choir: or hastens without delay to the common labour of the community; then in the garden of his heart by the grace of the Holy Ghost fresh flowers begin to arise, to grow and to become glorious with the fruits of obedience: and they shall be reckoned to him unto very great merit and the more beauteous adorning of his crown. But the lover of solitude and the contemplator of devout meditation must be on his guard against frivolities and rumours: lest by long occupation and unnecessary conversations he lose the sweetness of the mystic ointment: and a slight infection of vinegar and gall destroy the taste of honey. For who is so devout in prayer, so studious in holy reading, so strenuous in toil; who so speedily recollects himself within; as easily as he inclines to things exterior? Who so quickly mends what has been broken; as easily as he breaks anything? Who so soon cleans away stains; as easily as he falls into filth? Therefore O virgins of Christ, O religious servants of God: stand upon guard over your heart and mouth; lest your senses be corrupted by various desires of the world: which bring no profit to them that walk therein with many dangers and distresses. Behold with numberless deceits and snares: the world is full. Therefore according to the word of Christ, it behoveth to watch and pray against temptations and tribulations arising from every side: and not to fail in well doing as long as strength is there and the time for meriting grace abounds. For it is not a matter of losing a shoe lace, to forfeit the grace of God: to neglect the time of penance: to spend the days idly: and to spurn everlasting life for a little pleasure. Think over the boundless goodness of Christ towards the human race, what great good things He did, what great evils He suffered: and what great rewards He has promised to His elect after the conflicts of this life. Have a good trust in the Lord always; and fly to the divine assistance in every need: and in the time of tribulation do not lose heart, nor cease from prayer. You may take a noteworthy example of patience and perseverance from St. Agnes, Christ's virgin and martyr: a child indeed in body, but an ancient in soul: small of stature, great in merits, weak in sex, most strong in faith: stripped of her garments, adorned with virtues: who to overcome the devil and his fellows: fled to Christ with devout and earnest prayers. And when the human rabble did not cease but by the instigation of the devil made ready a great fire; she biding fearless in the midst of the flames, prayed with outstretched hands: praised Christ with heart and mouth; and desired to attain by the palm of martyrdom her Bridegroom: Whom she loved above all with a most sincere love. For the boundless love of Christ was more mighty in one frail maiden: than the fury of the tyrant armed with sword and fire. Therefore did she merit to have this golden crown adorned with three flowering garlands; because she spurned the world, tamed the flesh: overcame the devil, mocked the tyrant: spurned rewards, conquered pains, and dying for Christ by a most blissful end attained the glory of Christ. Now let us all together pray and call on Our Lord Jesus Christ, the lover of chastity, of innocence and of all purity; that He teach us to imitate the angelic life in frail flesh: and with the holy virgins especially to love, venerate and preserve chastity of mind and body. Amen.

A PRAYER

O most sweet Lord Jesus Christ, flower of all virtues, most chaste lover of virgins, most mighty foe of the demons, most unrelenting extirpator of vices, graciously look upon my weakness, and by the intercession of Thy most blessed Mother the Virgin Mary, and of Thy beloved Bride St. Agnes, venerable virgin and martyr, grant me the aid of heavenly strength that I may learn to despise all earthly things, and to love heavenly, to resist vice, and not to yield to temptations, firmly to cleave to virtue, to flee honours, to shun pleasures, to mourn past sins, to avoid the occasions of evil, to refrain from bad habits, to converse with the good and to persevere in good, that by the gift of Thy grace I may merit to possess the crown of eternal life with St. Agnes and all Thy saints for ever in Thy kingdom. Amen.

AN EXAMPLE

A certain brother of our house often suffered from headache: and he was therefore sometimes obliged to leave the choir. But he had a special devotion to the venerable virgin St. Agnes our Patroness: overflowing with the sweetness of much compassion. And so he desired with great eagerness of heart to visit her holy relics at Utrecht: which are preserved there with honour in the Cathedral Church of St. Martin in a silver casket covered with gold. It came to pass therefore that he went with his Prior to visit the aforesaid place of great veneration and arriving at the above mentioned Cathedral which is fitly adorned with many relics of saints: he begged the sacristan that the casket of most blessed Agnes should be shown him which he had long desired to see in the vehemence of his devotion. Then the guardian of the sacred relics replied: "I may not easily open the precious casket of St. Agnes; but I will willingly show you the ancient reliquary of the holy virgin: in which her sacred relics long rested to the praise and honour of God." And hearing this the brother was glad and consoled: awaiting until the venerable casket should be presented to him. And when it was seen and opened; he reverently bowed and kissed the holy case, and placed his head inside it with confidence: hoping that by the merits of St. Agnes relief would be at once given him. This done therefore he rendered most heartfelt thanks to God and the virgin St. Agnes: that with his own open eyes he had merited to see these things. From which time and henceforth he was not only delivered from the former pains in the body: but also he made progress in soul in great devotion; and closed well the remainder of his life by a sweet and happy death in fervour of spirit.

ANOTHER

When another brother had been reading in the refectory on the eve of St. Agnes; it befell him by accident that as he was afterwards taking his meal alone a fish bone broke in his mouth and so firmly stuck in his palate: that he could neither draw out nor spit out its point. Wherefore becoming very sad, and fearing that loss of voice threatened him from this injury: he awaited patiently for the Vespers of St. Agnes which were to be solemnly sung in choir. And when the cantor had commenced aloud the responsary Pulcbra facie: and the assembled choir with joyous voice continued the rest devoutly singing and praising to the honour of St. Agnes; the injured brother also began to sing, and suppliantly to invoke St. Agnes his beloved and kind Patroness: that she would succour him in this hour and free him from this misfortune. And, O wondrous clemency of God and how ineffable is His virtue and power: Who forsakes not them that hope in Him from whatsoever trouble they shall call upon Him. For as soon as he sang these words with the choir, Intercede pro nobis omnibus: he felt a little tickling in the palate of the throat, and he began to cough a little: and in a moment with the saliva of his mouth he spat out the fish bone without any harm to his throat. Then being made very joyful he gave thanks to God and the virgin St. Agnes: that he had merited to be heard and cured so speedily. And when Vespers were over, he remained silently in the choir, prostrating himself humbly upon her footstool, kissing the wooden pedestal from inmost affection of heart: congratulating himself in secret upon so great a benefit vouchsafed him by the merits of St. Agnes. Then wishing to assure himself more of the actual fact; he looked for the fish bone which had dropped from his mouth: and he found it fallen on the floor. Taking it with him to his cell, he set it near a picture of St. Agnes: as a perpetual reminder of her special love. By whose holy patronage may the merciful Lord deign to defend us from every danger always and everywhere: and to keep us in a good way with all those commended to us in prayer. Amen.

ANOTHER

There was in the city of Zwolle a certain citizen by name Hermann de Oever, a rich and honourable man, compassionate and merciful towards the poor: and a faithful procurator of the sick and the needy in the hospital of the Holy Ghost. He on the occasion of a certain disturbance in the city against him and some other fellow townsmen: fled to our monastery on the Mount of the virgin St. Agnes for shelter. And because of his worth and goodness he was received and treated kindly: with much charity and brotherly goodwill. And after a short time had passed, he learnt to say the Confiteor and to serve the priest at Mass: although he was now an old man and quite ignorant of letters. And this he did with such diligence and devotion: that when others were otherwise occupied he would willingly and cheerfully serve priests at Mass two or three times in one day. And it was especially our venerable Father William Vorniken, at that time Prior of our house, a special lover of St. Agnes: that he often served with great affection, clothed in a surplice behind in the Church during the High Mass, while the choir was singing.

But it happened one day that he lost some money out of the cell where he dwelt: over which he was very much grieved wondering who had done this. For he had not yet resigned his own: but he lived among the brethren within the cloister as a guest and faithful friend. For during the midday meal some one, a stranger and unknown, secretly entered his cell by the open window: robbed as much as he pleased and quickly departed. When dinner was over and Hermann after the thanksgiving entered his cell; looking for his money he did not find it: and very much saddened he said complaining to one of the lay brothers, Brother John de Eme with whom he was familiar: "O good dear brother John, are there thieves here in the house?" Who said: "Certainly not, good Hermann." Then he made known the theft that had been committed on him saying: "I have lost the money which I had in my cell: and which has now been secretly stolen during dinner." To whom brother John comforting the distressed man replied: "Do not think, good friend, that any of our brothers or of the servants of this house has done this. But haply some strange visitor who entered the orchard, being tempted has done it: as we have sometimes experienced before when clothing has been secretly stolen." But hearing these things our venerable Father and Prior William was exceedingly sad: and all the brethren grieved for the loss of the good man from shame for the theft. Then some of our brothers better known to him comforting and encouraging him to patience, said to him: "O most dear Hermann be patient now in this: for haply Our Lord God does not wish that you trouble your heart any more about this money. You should make then now a virtue of necessity: and offer it to God and St. Agnes for the salvation of your soul. And if afterwards it befall you to get it again; that you do not wish to keep back any of it: but that all should go to the worship of God and the service of St. Agnes." He did with a good soul and a pious intention what was counselled him: freely vowing everything to God, and the blessed Virgin Mary, and St. Agnes the Patroness of our Church, which had been consecrated a short while before. When this votive offering had been accomplished: after three days there came a good messenger from Zwolle sent by Master John Haerlem then rector of the devout Beguin Sisters saying: "Brethren, be not anxious and troubled for the lost money: with the favour of God you will soon receive it again." Hearing this Hermann rejoiced: and with him our Prior and the whole community. But who the thief and burglar was, a cleric or a layman: is still unknown. For it is hoped that he repented, and secretly begged Master John to send it all back to the monastery: which also he faithfully did without mentioning any name. But with this money regained two sets of vestments were bought and made to the honour of

St. Agnes: and one silver gilt chalice inscribed with the title Hermann de Oever on the foot of the chalice.

ANOTHER

A certain brother of our house celebrating in the Chapter House at the altar of the virgin St Agnes, by the snare of the devil was on a sudden tempted during Mass concerning the faith and the sacrament of the body of Christ: wherein very often he had great consolation and devotion. Feeling therefore that a grave question was arising: he turned himself speedily to the merciful Lord Jesus Christ with groaning and a right intention of faith praying. And at once he heard within a divine answer addressed to him. "Believe thou as St. Agnes, Caecilia, Barbara, and other holy virgins believed: who suffered for Christ and doubted of no doctrine of faith." When he heard this: the temptation ceased and the questioning doubt. And very often afterwards he turned over these words against any suggestion of the devil: "Believe as Agnes, Caecilia, and Barbara: and thou shalt never err in the Catholic Faith. For there are as many true witnesses: as there are holy words in the Bible."

ANOTHER

Another also of our brothers communicated out of devotion at the same place and altar: he was infirm and had long been accustomed to walk bowed down, supporting himself on crutches. But after the celebration of the Mass by the power of Christ, and the merits of St. Agnes, he became so strong: that he left his crutches there after the Mass: and then passed to the choir and the community rejoicing and upright. And a certain brother being astonished at this event: piously began to question: what the sick man had done and thought during the Mass. And the man who was healed replied: "I thought and turned over the words of the holy Gospel: which Luke narrates of Our Lord Jesus Christ: 'And the whole multitude sought to touch Him: and virtue went out from Him, and healed all.' " A good faith then and the power of the sacraments with the prayers of the saints can still heal the weak in mind and body; that they may become fervent in the love of God, and more ready for every good work: and obedient to their prelates without delay. These be the miracles of eternal salvation: which Christ in His great clemency still often works with the devout.

ANOTHER

It happened likewise once in Lent that a certain brother was asked to celebrate Mass about the fifth hour in the morning for the guests and the whole family of our household; as was usual for the good custody of those who laboured in the offices: and for those setting out on a journey near or far. And that brother piously agreed: and from charity willingly did as he was requested. It was then the feast of St. Gregory, Pope, whom the brother loved with a special devotion: because on his feast he first entered the school to learn the alphabet with other children. When therefore he had arrived at the altar he began to think what Mass he should say: of the fast or of St. Gregory. It immediately entered his mind, "Thou hast not yet said the Mass of St. Agnes this week: for the special cause commended to thee. Read now therefore the Mass of St. Agnes with the collect of St. Gregory: and afterwards thou shalt sing his Mass in the choir with the whole community with a gladsome heart." He did so therefore with a good confidence: fulfilling his vow to St. Agnes our Patroness most highly beloved of Christ. While then nearly all were gathered in the Church and were hearing Mass: there befell the danger of a great fire in our farm house, unknown to any one. But the loving and merciful Lord saw to it very well: that the fire was speedily quenched. For a certain lay oblate of ours by name Matthias, going out of the Church after the elevation, came upon the spot: and put out the commencement of the fire. The which we are confident should be ascribed to the merits of St. Agnes: of whom in particular at that time a Mass was being read, to beseech the Lord for a pious cause. For God Who preserved blessed Agnes unharmed praying in the midst of the flames with outstretched hands: He on that day in loving goodness saved our house with all its utensils unburnt by her prayers and merits. For one of the laics entered the Church with the others to hear Mass; and he had neglected to put out a lantern under the roof of the house: which, having burnt its cord, fell upon the straw lying there and set it on fire. But the compassionate Lord seeing all and heeding in mercy the prayers of the poor: vouchsafed that this danger should be met by another in good time as was said above. And our devout and dearly loved Father, Brother Theodoric Clive, the third venerable Prior of our house, hearing that the danger of fire had befallen, and by the favour of God had immediately ceased: at first was seized with terror: and no wonder. Then he was comforted and gave thanks to God that so grave a peril had not spread: but had been at once removed. When then the news of the fire reached the ears of the others: the brother who on the same day celebrated the Mass of St. Agnes, went privately to his Father Prior: and humbly told him: "Dear Father let us give thanks to God and St. Agnes our Patroness: because her Mass was read to-day for a special cause: and I am sure that she prayed for us, and the Lord delivered us from that fire." Then the good father and pious shepherd rejoicing greatly, as a chaste lover of St. Agnes, enjoined special prayers upon the brethren; and ordered that greater alms should be distributed to the poor: for so marked a protection from the fire at the time, and from all evil to come. Amen.

ANOTHER

A certain man stole a horse from the pasturage of our monastery of Mt. St. Agnes; which he took with him beyond a mile from our monastery: thinking that he was safe and that he would return prosperously to his home with his spoils. Coming therefore to a certain town he bound the horse with a cord to a post in the hedge at a cross road: and entering an inn sat there to drink and rest a little. Meanwhile, however, the horse standing outside alone, and seeing nobody there, becoming somewhat restless, because he was in a strange district, and violently taken away from the place of his dwelling: began to move his head constantly hither and thither, and to kick with his heels. And he tugged so long this way and that at the rein with which he had been bound: that at last he broke the knot of the fastening. And when he found himself free and untied, and waiting a long time did not see his rider: and because it is natural to an animal tied up to love liberty and to return to his accustomed stable: he at once turned his head to the straight road by which he had come: and running swiftly alone by the leading of God arrived safe at the monastery gate. And standing quietly there and awaiting in the place known to him: he was easily recognized by our porter and farm labourer, and gladly brought in: for which may God be blessed for ever.

O most blessed Agnes ever worthy of honour, we attribute this to thy merits: because in many of our needs we have experienced thy patronage. Therefore we proclaim and devoutly invoke and praise Christ in thee: giving thanks to God always for all His blessings mercifully bestowed upon us. Amen.

SERMON XXVIII

ON THE DEDICATION OF THE CHURCH: OF THE FIVE LAMPS OF THE TEMPLE

MY house shall be called the house of prayer, saith the Lord. Beloved brethren, to-day is the solemn festival of the dedication of our Church; which ought to be devoutly and joyously celebrated by all dwelling in this place: and which ought to uplift the minds of those who keep it to the heavenly bliss of the angels. For unto this is every Church built and dedicated: that therein the worship of divine praise be performed: and the prayers of the faithful merit to be more speedily and fully heard by God in the holy place. Now the Church of God is much adorned and illuminated: if these following five acts of worship be exercised therein: and as heavenly lamps be carefully kept that they may give light in the temple of God.

The first that shines forth among other acts of divine worship and lights up the house of prayer: and excites those that enter the Church to pray, and enkindles the hearts of the faithful in divine love; is when priests clothed with the sacred vestments, reverently go up to the altar, devoutly celebrate Masses: and for themselves and for the common people offer the sacrifice supremely pleasing to God, and piously intercede.

The second that chiefly adorns the house of God and gives splendour to the choirs of clerics: is when the canonical Hours instituted by the Church are daily duly rendered in their seasons by clerics and religious: and all things that are to be recited and sung are reverently and beseemingly performed and accomplished to the honour of God: and all levity, noise and disorder are as far as possible strictly avoided.

The third which brings exceeding beauty and light to the house of God: is when the word of God is frequently preached with fervour by priests, pastors and doctors to the Christian people, to kings and princes, to old and young, to small and great, and they are terrified as by a heavenly trumpet with punishments not to sin: and are comforted with eternal rewards not to despair. For holy priests and preachers shall have great rewards, who instruct many by their life and teaching: and by frequent admonition draw and lead them to virtue. Whence of our holy Father Augustine the glorious doctor of holy Church we read and sing: that he preached the word of God in the holy Church unceasingly, readily and mightily, with sound mind and clear intelligence even to his last illness. Who by the help of God lived long in virtue for the salvation of many writing books and teaching the ignorant: and he magnificently enriched, adorned and enlightened holy Church by the multitude of his books. Whom for the excellence of his merits it is right to praise: and with filial affection ever to honour and suppliantly to beseech; that we may be able to follow him on the right path to Christ reigning in Heaven: Whom he so burningly loved and praised in hymns and psalms while he was on earth.

Fourthly the house of God is much beautified and brightened by frequent visiting of the Church to hear the word of God: and to keep the law of life and discipline which leads to the country of eternal radiance and peace. For those who desire happily to attain after death the joys of the heavenly kingdom: should now while they are in health and life, frequently visit the house of God, and willingly hear sermons: often make confession, seek and pray for indulgences. Time is short: and the hour of health uncertain. He therefore who now does not repent and amend; after the door is shut shall stand without and shall not obtain mercy: he shall cry mourning, nor shall he be heard when he weeps. Happy the people and very praiseworthy: which leaving vain sights, hastens betimes to the house of prayer and to the preaching of the divine word: giving thanks to God for blessings received: and praying for more to come. A beautiful sight: to see the temple of God on all sides full of the faithful: and the market at rest from the business of the world.

Fifthly the Church of God is decked and illumined by the frequent and common prayer of many, both of the clergy and of the whole Christian people, urgently beseeching God: for the divers intentions and needs of all in want, sound and sick, living and dead. These five lamps are very necessary and useful in every Church; they excellently adorn the house of prayer: and as five burning lights illuminate the temple of God: and show the right way to the Jerusalem above and the heavenly dwelling. Wherever therefore in the Church these devout and holy offices are reverently and diligently performed in their due time: there God dwells, there He presides, teaches and rules: as blessed John says in the Apocalypse: "Behold the tabernacle of God with men: and He will dwell with them." Having therefore shut out all noise and gossip with jesting: it is befitting and right to do naught else in the house of prayer and the holy place; save what most pleases God and edifies the neighbours: and belongs especially to the divine worship. What things then that aid the grace of devotion, and the sweetness of the canticles and the understanding of the words: these should be weighed in the heart, and with rejoicing mouth uttered to the praise of God. All vicious and idle discourses are everywhere to be shunned: but nevertheless especially in the temple of God, in the court of the sovereign King, in the sanctuary of the Holy Ghost, in the sight of the angels and the heavenly citizens, in the presence of the spirits above. Highly venerable therefore is this place foreseen from eternity by God, and chosen and set aside to serve Him with His ministers and sacred vessels: and in the time preordained, by the hands of the Bishop consecrated and adorned with many holy relics. In which place indeed human things are united with divine, the lowest with the highest, earthly with heavenly: through the sacraments of Christ which are there handled and celebrated by the priests in Masses. What the holy angels do in Heaven, this also the faithful ought to do on earth: to wit, praise and bless God with all their strength: and magnify Him above all saints and creatures, for His gifts and blessings. And if not with such dignity and cheerfulness as the angels: nevertheless ever yone should strive to do according to the power of his weakness and fit himself, that he may always praise God perfectly with the angels: love Him above all, and in all things bless. If thou canst not make music with the lips of thy mouth: thou shouldst cry to God with the sighs of the heart. If thou art hoarse or unmelodious, cease not from praise: nor withdraw from the divine worship; but listen to what is sung and recited by others: and rejoice with them that sing well. If thou canst not sing so beautifully as the larks and nightingales: sing and praise mournfully like the crows and the frogs in the marsh: who sing as God has given and nature has allowed. Be not puffed up, jackdaw, for the loudness of thy voice: for thou knowest not how long thou shalt last and sing high. The voice indeed of a humble and contrite heart: sounds well in the ears of God almighty, Who hears all things. Sing and praise God in the voice of exultation, mindful nevertheless of thy own vileness with fear of trouble to come. Sing humbly with holy David in the psalm: "Let my heart rejoice that it may fear Thy name." Who so faithful in all things as David going forth at the bidding of the king; who was a soldier by day fighting valiantly, a monk by night rising cheerfully and praying devoutly? If thou canst not with St. John the evangelist contemplate things lofty and divine: fall down with Mary Magdalene at the feet of Jesus humbly imploring pardon and weeping for thy sins: that thou mayest receive remission of the many sins, whereby thou hast often offended God. If thou canst not with St. Paul fly to the third Heaven: thou shouldst remain with him by Jesus crucified, not glorying in the flesh: but crucifying the flesh with its vices and concupiscences. If thou hast not the wings of an eagle which flies to the stars of Heaven; have the wings of the simple dove which builds her nest in the rock: daily meditating the most holy wounds of Jesus. For humble Francis found more holiness and sweetness in the Passion of Christ: than a subtle astronomer in gazing upon the stars of Heaven. Forsaking therefore things vain and useless, study in the Life and Passion of Christ: and it will profit thee more than all the arts of the world. If thou wishest to be comforted from Heaven: flee men and the news of the world. Be willingly alone with the Lord: and seek solace within in devout prayers and holy meditations. Nothing is more wholesome, nothing sweeter, nothing more pleasant; than to praise God in hymns and psalms: and to have the heart aloft with the angels in Heaven, leaving aside all things below. Such a one may say in rapture of spirit: "I was mindful of God alone in the joy of my heart." Truly the Lord is in this place: this is naught else but the house of God and the gate of Heaven. Open to me the gates, ye holy angels: and I will sing with you the name of the Lord my God for ever and ever. But woe to him, who knowingly thinks of vain things amid divine: and with a perverse mind turns over things offensive. Woe to him who fancies unclean idols: and neglects the precious wounds of Christ: and fears not to suffer the torments of hell. Woe to him who there is silent and sleeps: where he ought to watch and pray. Woe to the idle and dissolute, and to the late comers; who look round the walls with roving eyes: and heed not the sweet psalms. Woe to them that often think of food and drink: and consider little and rarely mourn for the pains of the souls in Purgatory. If any one was there for an hour he would never feel weariness in choir: nor sadness in fasting: nor fatigue in toil. Blessed all religious and devout servants of God, cheerful in divine worship, studious in reading and writing books: who restrain themselves and others from light words: and faithfully pray for their benefactors and all the troubled and tempted: whose number is very great: better known to God than to men. Whoever then is thankful and faithful in small and present gifts: he shall be worthy to receive greater from God in Heaven. To do aught negligently in the Divine Office: will not go unpunished. Take care and fear lest the alms cry out against you that they have been ill spent: and the Hours often heedlessly recited and accomplished. From which evils may Jesus Christ deliver us; forgive us all our trespasses: and after the perils of this life happily lead us to the heavenly kingdoms. Amen.

SERMON XXIX

OF THE ORNAMENTS AND VIRTUES OF THE MINISTERS IN THE TEMPLE OF GOD

THEY adorned the front of the temple with crowns of gold; and they dedicated the altar to the Lord: and there was great joy among the people. Beloved brethren, these things are read in the first Book of the Macchabees, concerning the renewed temple of God: and they are also sung by us in the Church at the accustomed time. As therefore those saints of old were joyous and devout in the material temple, praising God in hymns and organs, for the victory given them from Heaven over their foes: so we also ought to be much more devout giving thanks to Christ Who has delivered us from the tumult of the world and the snares of the devil; and has given us hope of attaining the festivity of the heavenly Jerusalem: and the dedication of the immaterial temple where God dwells with all His saints. You should seek in the letter the spiritual sense, and in the wax the hidden honey; and let your soul rejoice in the living God, and in every word which proceedeth from the mouth of God: as the angels and all the saints in Heaven. For then shall your soul be able to ascend by the ladder of the holy words to the heights of Heaven: when it heeds not outward beauty; and from its inmost heart is mindful of the Lord its God alone: as far as it is given it to taste of the grace of supernal visitation in the state of human weakness.

Brothers, there is great rejoicing in the dedication of the Church there: where there is the purity of an innocent life, the freedom of a good conscience, the gladness of spiritual joy; the preaching of a holy doctrine, the observance of the regular discipline: remembrance of the heavenly kingdom, forgetfulness of all worldly joy. There is true beauty of the temple, and adorning of the Church with boughs and sweet smelling flowers there; where there is true contrition of heart, humble confession of mouth: and worthy satisfaction for sins committed. There is the joyous dedication of a new altar there: where there is fresh fervour of devotion with giving of thanks in rejoicing of heart for blessings received.

No one should appear empty in the sight of the Lord: but each should always have something to offer at the altar to the honour of God. He offers a calf and a goat: who crushes the wantonness of the flesh by fasting. He slays a bull and an ox: who brings down the pride of mind and the obstinacy of his own opinion to nothing by humility and the counsel of the wise. He offers a spotless lamb worthy of God; who daily devoutly commemorates the Passion of Christ: and conforms himself to Him by patience and mildness. He sacrifices a ram; who ascribes all his virtue and strength to God: and attributes nothing of good to himself. He burns the loins, the heart and the breast upon the altar: who curbs all carnal affections by the fervour of a holy spirit. He offers a dove: who walks in simplicity, and holds his peace concerning the affairs of others; who mourns with the sorrowing: and prays for them that contradict him. He offers a turtle dove to God: who loves chastity and seeks solitude; and when he loses earthly solace: flies the more freely to the heavenly palace. He sacrifices a sparrow: who abstains from the chattering of useless words; and dwells alone in the secret of his cell that he may have greater peace: and be burdensome to none by speech. And he adorns the front of the temple with crowns of gold; who willingly reads, writes and preaches the noble deeds of the saints: and to the encouragement of virtue proclaims their rewards to others, that they fail not in temptations. He hangs up golden shields in the Church for adornment; who relates to his neighbours with what great virtues the fathers of the Old and New Testament are resplendent unto their edification; who recites the conflicts of the martyrs unto the bearing of adversity: commemorates the toils of confessors unto abstinence: beatifies the trophies of virgins and the continence of widows unto the chastising of the body: worthily praises the books of the doctors and the sermons of preachers unto studying, reading, writing: and unfolds and explains the good works of others unto the praise of God and the honour of Holy Church. He paints and adorns beautiful pictures: who edifies his neighbour by his life and conduct. Behold so many golden escutcheons shine in the church; as there are names of saints, as festivals, as holy words: as we see good examples.

O what a great festival is celebrated in the Church triumphant; where having overcome all enemies all the saints rejoice together with the holy angels clothed in white robes: and crowned with golden crowns that shall never perish. There indeed there is eternal praise and glory: that shall abide without ceasing. There the voice is sweet without harshness; the singing high without fatigue: peace boundless without fear; joy without grief, love without envy, knowledge without error. There there is abundance without want, dignity without contempt: health without death; bliss without weeping, security without fear: pleasure without vice, fullness without weariness; brightness without shadow, truth without ambiguity: purity without stain, freedom without hindrance; conscience without scruple, supreme happiness without end: all good things in God. O how festively rejoice there the souls of the saints loosed from the bond of the body, cleansed from all stain of sin: intimately united with God, one with Him without a medium, flying freely through the space of Heaven: singing and giving thanks to God most joyfully. "The snare is broken: and we are delivered."

As often therefore as there is any feast of the saints in the Church; we ought to remember what and how great it is in Heaven: and despise everything that gives pleasure in this life. Happy the religious who apart from all worldly crowds: free from temporal cares, and at rest from the passions: direct the eye of the mind to heavenly things: and for the sweetness of the interior love which they feel, desire to be dissolved and to be with Christ. Happy those who are called to the heavenly dedication and to the supper of the Lamb: and so strive to prepare themselves, that they may be worthy to enter with the elect. A true saying: "No man can rejoice here with the world: and afterwards reign with Christ." Pleasant meadows lead the unwise to evil shelters. And those who now always seek delights and honours: after brief joy shall find eternal fire and grief. Alas miserable and foolish lovers of the world; who turn the feasts of Christ and the honours of the saints into banquets of feasting and games; where shall ye abide? Woe to you who abandon Jesus, and seek the world: neglect the saints, and associate to yourselves the dissipated and dissolute; displease the angels, and rejoice the demons. Woe to you who mock the simple and praise the deceitful; tread under foot the roses of virtue, and gather the thorns of sin; gaze upon present goods and foresee not nor fear the evils to come. Why, fools, do ye deceive yourselves; and return not to the right way? Fear God lest at any time the Lord be angry, and you perish speedily from the earth with the wicked: and receive hell for the pleasures which you loved. For the labourer is worthy of his hire: whether he has done well or ill in this life.

Our happy and holy mother the Church has also for her great comfort and for the beauty of the house of God in good custody many bodies of saints: worthy of all honour. At the sight of which many faithful are often excited to the love of God and tears; earnestly beseeching their daily intercession: that by their holy merits they may merit to attain everlasting joys. For what church is there or chapel so poor and small; that has not or does not succeed in obtaining some holy relics for the adornment of its sanctuary: and for devotion to the souls of the saints reigning with Christ in glory? For humbly to venerate the sacred bones of the saints, is to honour Christ: since in them the Holy Ghost dwelt; by them the world was overcome: and the devil put to shame through the faith of Christ. We must trust therefore without hesitation that they will willingly pray for us their friends dwelling upon earth; whom they see fervent in prayer, and often raising the eyes with groaning to Heaven: and forsaking all things from the heart for Christ's sake. It also aids weak souls not a little to gladness of heart: if on feasts priests and ministers are clad in better vestments and copes to celebrate the divine worship with more solemnity; if the altars and holy places are adorned with flowers and foliage: so that by outward signs the hearts of the slow may be enkindled the more speedily to meditate upon heavenly things. However in these ceremonies, services and ornaments naught should be done vainly for human praise and one's own complacency; lest God, Who regards the hearts of the humble, be offended by useless clamour and dissolute conduct: lest the temporal feast be changed into a sin for the soul from some levity or curiosity. For praise is not seemly in the mouth of a proud man; nor does God take pleasure in sonorous lips, tainted with vain-glory: or opened with discordant voice. Let then every devout suppliant give thanks to God: let every ardent lover sing praises to the Lord; let all the souls of the saints with the angels in Heaven chant and praise God: let all the churches of earth with the faithful in this world chant and praise God saying: "Praise and honour beseem Thee, O Lord: for Thy exceeding great majesty for ever and ever. Amen."

SERMON XXX

OF THE FOUR CONDITIONS BELONGING TO THE BUILDING AND BEAUTY OF THE HOUSE OF GOD

HOLINESS becometh Thy house, O Lord: unto length of days. Beloved brethren, be ye circumspect and guarded in every time and place; but especially in the Church, in the choir and at the Divine Office: where you may be remarked by many. You are the temple of God, you are the house of God: God has chosen you unto His inheritance, to whom He has promised to give the kingdom of God. Note therefore the four conditions that belong to the beauty of the house of God: and lead to the holiness of true religion. Every good house ought to have a strong foundation: straight walls; bright windows: and a whole roof.

First the house of our soul ought to have the foundation of a deep humility: lest the whole building fall from the height of pride into the abyss of eternal damnation. Therefore have many fallen away from the religious state into divers temptations of the devil and sins of the flesh: because they had not nor took their stand upon the strong foundation of true humility: which guards a man from numberless snares of the devil and falls. Happy the soul that desires not temporal honour; but shuns all ease as much as it can: and deems contempt the greatest gain. Said a certain devout man: "They who praise me oft deceive me; and they who blame me: often do me good." Whence holy David prays: "Let not the foot of pride come to me." Why? "For there the workers of iniquity are fallen: they are cast out, and could not stand." And why could they not stand? Because they were proud: and gave not thanks to God. "For God resisteth the proud: but to the humble He giveth grace." For no man is safely and rightly praised, but the truly humble: to whom the world is as faded and all its glory. He then who will stand well and firmly, let him hold to the foundation of humility: let him depart not from humility: however much he may be praised, or honoured. Take care brethren that ye lose not the whole reward of your labour through pride and the empty praise of men: that ye fall not with the devil into damnation and everlasting fire. For speedily as smoke passes away all pleasure of the flesh, all temporal honour and glory; but the pain of hell shall not pass away speedily: nay that sulphurous fire prepared for the wicked shall last for ever.

Secondly the house of our soul ought to have four walls straight and strong, standing upright and welded; not of crooked beams and broken joists, but of precious stones skilfully squared and well polished. These are the four holy gospels written with truth concerning the incarnation of Christ: wholesomely designed for the whole world unto a right belief and a just and pious living. These walls are as most strong outworks: and as the towers of Jerusalem with their ramparts; which cannot fall or perish for ever: because the truth of the Lord is from ever and shall abide even unto eternity. However much then the world may rage against the humble and devout faithful; or the devil tempt, or the tyrant persecute or the greedy despoil: the just man nevertheless trusting in the Lord shall not be disturbed. And if the malignant curse, the pagan scoff, the Jew mock, the cunning argue, the philosopher reject: the incredulous doubt, the heretic err, the blasphemous snarl, the possessed clamour: the furious terrify with swords, the mad tear with the teeth: nevertheless against lying men the truth-telling Christ shall ever prevail: and with Him shall be victorious the faithful Christian who is strengthened by His words of truth. "Fear not," he saith, "little flock. For I will give you a mouth and wisdom: which all your adversaries will not be able to resist and gainsay. For it is easier for Heaven and earth to pass: than one tittle of the law to fall." He therefore who follows Christ, and believes rightly and lives well, as the gospels teach and the holy doctors fully expound: he has four walls straight and strong welded by divine charity: which firmly fortify the temple of his soul: and drive away all doubts from his mind. For thus are the words of the holy gospel divinely inspired in the faithful man and the devout soul: as a golden shield against the fiery temptations of the devil and the flatteries of the flesh; as the precious stones on the breast of Aaron the priest against the errors of the world: as white pearls on the crown of a virgin against wicked thoughts; as burning lamps in the midst of the Church most brightly gleaming before the Lord of Heaven and earth: and as columns of bronze adorned with silver sustaining the whole building of the temple.

Happy the soul to which is pleasant and sweet every word that proceedeth from the mouth of God: and whatever she hears or reads in the gospel of Christ. For the more often a man hears and reads the words of the gospel: and the more heedfully he considers and muses upon them: the more progress shall he make in virtue: and the more firmly shall the house of his soul stand and the more brightly shall it be resplendent. Much also shall he rejoice in the end who loves Jesus intimately: and he shall receive a special grace from Him because of his mindfulness of Him. For He Himself saith to His beloved disciples: exiled in the world: "Abide in My love. He that abideth in Me and I in him: the same beareth much fruit." If you wish to bear much fruit and to increase the merit of your labours: then go by the narrow way forsaking your own will for the sake of obedience: which leads by a straight path to eternal life. If you would also know the sum total of all books, then strive to follow Christ by the cross and contempt of all worldly things; and you shall find rest for your souls: and the kingdom of Heaven shall be opened to you.

Clear then the field of your heart from the briars and thorns of vices: and you shall receive the grace of Christ and the friendship of all the holy angels. For assuredly while you labour in the vineyard of the Lord many kinds of virtue shall spring up in your soul: to wit, for the burdock of pride, the spikenard of humility: for the nettle of lust, the lily of chastity: for the wormwood of anger, the fig of mildness; for the thorn of envy, the rose of charity: for the briar of gloom, the mugwort of spiritual joy; for the cockle of discord, the balsam of sweet agreement: for the juniper of injury, the olive of brotherly compassion: for the berry of dissipation: the myrrh of devout meditation.

Thirdly, the house of our soul ought to have seven bright windows always open to receive the light of Heaven from God: but shut against the thunders and thunderbolts of the devil. These windows are the seven gifts of the Holy Ghost; which illumine the soul by the knowledge of truth: and enkindle it within by the heat of charity. When these gifts are received and kindled the darkness of sin is dispelled, and the pleasures of the outward senses; which blind the eyes of those who look upon worldly vanities: who alas neglect the glory of the blessed in the kingdom of Heaven. Great care then must be taken that the windows of our soul be not darkened by the smoke of anger, or the cloud of gloom: or the dust of vainglory, or by an immodest fancy: or by long conversation. Especially must we watch that our windows, lit up by the spirit of wisdom and understanding in the scriptures, be not broken by hard words; or befouled by the mud of evil suspicion: or too much enfolded in temporal cares; and so turned away from the brightness of the heavenly light: and often deprived of heavenly consolation. Very carefully then must the windows of our house be guarded in every place and time because of the weakness of human life: which easily declines from the fervour of devotion to earthly occupations for recreation or under pretext of the profit of others. But the angel of Satan often beguiles him who takes leisure in God: under pretext of external recreation. And therefore we should insist the more on devout prayers: and protect the windows of our house the more strongly by holy meditations; lest the devil have an entry by the wandering of our mind: and this especially in time of prayer and study of spiritual reading. For Satan comes secretly by the door of the sight or hearing with external imaginations seeking to snatch the psalm or word from the mouth of him who recites: or urging to leave the choir from weariness of mind. Wherefore a great effort must be made and we must return betimes to interior things; that when Christ comes and knocks at the door it may be at once opened to Him: and the light of His grace sweetly flow in: and light up, cleanse and sanctify the whole house of the mind: and the more carefully guard and defend it from all inrushing vices.

O most gentle Lord Jesus Christ, my mercy and my refuge in my every tribulation and distress: O would Thou wouldst deign sometime to enter the house of my soul with heavenly light in the company of the angels: and with a golden thurible full of spices incense all my interior, and consecrate my heart as a temple of the Holy Ghost: sign it with the holy cross, anoint it with the oil of grace: place there the golden urn with manna, and firmly fix the book of Thy law to my side: that therein I may study Thy heavenly and divine commandments day and night: as long as I dwell an exile on this earth. The house of our soul should also have four strong beams: lest the walls be shaken by the wind of pride: or lest a man being struck by the arrow of malediction depart from the truth of the gospel and the holiness of a humble life. For all things without humility and a constant watchfulness: lie open to danger and ruin. Let the faithful soul then hold on to the beam of justice, doing injury to no man: let her hold on to the beam of fortitude, piously enduring the malice of others; let her hold on to the beam of temperance, curbing the wantonness of the flesh: let her hold on to the beam of prudence, being on her guard against the deceit of error. Also be not negligent: for negligence is the loss of much good work and time. Who shall easily regain time lost? One hour of silence spent with God rejoices the conscience more: than three hours spent in vain gossip. Be therefore, most beloved, diligent in labour: guarded in mouth: simple in evil: prudent in good: devout to God, kind to the neighbour: strangers to the world, near to Heaven.

Fourthly the house of our soul ought to have a roof solid and whole against the rain and wind; lest the work well begun perish before the end be completed: and he incur scandal who from heedlessness omitted to roof the house which was well founded. The Spouse says in the Canticles: "The beams of our houses are of cedar: our rafters of cypress trees." The rafters are made of two beams: which are joined at the top of the house and divided below: but fixed to the walls by nails. Let the soul therefore have constancy at the beginning of her conversion to make progress in virtue; let her also hold on to perseverance in good work unto the going forth of life from the prison of the body: that she may gain for the brief toil of the combat the reward of everlasting blessedness. With these two beams of constancy and perseverance is formed and completed the roof of the faithful soul: which is made unto the image of the holy Trinity. Many begin fervently, but gradually grow lukewarm; they turn to exterior things: and neglect to finish what they have begun. The house of these has not a sound roof; therefore evil thoughts often enter which stain the conscience: and destroy the grace of devotion. At length when the wind of temptation fiercely blows, either they fall away from their good purpose: or they think of departing from their place, by the instigation of the devil. These then unless they bow to the counsel of their prelates: cannot long persevere with the good. Do not, frail man, depart from the religious state and from the holy congregation; but endure a little while: for the hope of eternal reward in heavenly joys. Stand firm in thy good purpose, listen humbly to advice; strive every day manfully, toil diligently: pray frequently, bear patiently, forgive willingly: wait with longanimity, hope trustfully, persevere constantly: and thou shalt be crowned by God with a crown of glory undoubtedly. "For he that shall persevere unto the end: he shall be saved." It is useful also to roof our house with tiles; lest the wind of pride blow: or the rain of carnal delight stain the conscience. The tiles are the examples and words of Christ: which teach us to resist the devil; and to take up good meditations against evil suggestions: and day and night to watch in prayer.

Happy the soul which merits to bring her life to a good end of perseverance; so that after many toils of body and sorrows of heart it may be able to say in the end what Christ said on the cross: "It is consummated." These few words said to the praise of God concerning the house and temple of the soul: many thanks should be rendered to God even for the least good word or thought inspired from above. Every holy place then should be held ever in reverence by us: on account of the many blessings which there are wont to be bestowed upon devout suppliants. For there the sinner penitent and praying obtains pardon: the just man giving thanks merits grace. There the poor man moaning and beseeching obtains alms: the rich man compassionating and giving merits the mercy of God. There the priest celebrating offers to God a sacrifice more worthy than all other sacrifice; praying and bending the knee for himself and many others: there he who hears Mass is often touched even to tears sorrowing within. There the devout suppliant during Mass thinks on the sacred Passion of Christ: there the pilgrim wayfarer about to journey by land

and sea receives a blessing: and a guide for a good way Jesus Christ the faithful friend. There the minister of the priest supplies the place of the angels, by a service most pleasing to God: there the communicant receives the most holy body of the Lord the food of angels the most noble of all gifts. There he who is going to toil for the day receives strength from God; the sorrowful receive consolation, the fearful courage: the compunct devotion. There the tempted find a remedy; the troubled counsel: the weak help. There the sound receive joy, the sick medicine: the dying a defence against the enemy on the way: the dead deliverance from pains, by the celebration of Masses. It is good therefore to enter the house of God, to visit the church: to hear Mass, to go round the cemetery, to pray for the dead: to worship the holy places and altars: to keep relics, to honour the images of the saints: above all the holy men and women to suppliantly adore the sacrament of Christ; not to discuss lofty things: to be unwilling to dive into difficult questions; humbly to respect mysteries: to commit deep matters to God. For the truth deceives no man: Almighty God can do all things. He who would stand well and please God: should grieve much over all his past offences: even for good neglected and sins confessed. It is the salvation of the soul often to moan, often to pray: often to confess, often to communicate. It is a sign of devotion often to make good resolutions, often to think good thoughts: often to write, read, muse on hymns and psalms: never to idle, to shun frivolities: to work things profitable: to love God with the heart and devoutly praise with the mouth.

Brethren, now is the time of grace: now we ought to seek, ask and knock: and fit ourselves by every effort to receive the grace of God. Now are we able every day and in every place to merit the eternal kingdom, and escape eternal pains: if by the grace of God we do true penance. The door of Heaven is not yet closed: the gate is open: those may enter who are ready. Those who are not ready let them strive to prepare themselves, and amend their life more perfectly: that when Christ comes and calls they may be worthy to enter joyfully with the just. O faithful and humble soul consider how great is the mercy of God over thee in all thy life: that He does not immediately avenge Himself: but waits long and lovingly recalls to Himself. O happy Mother Church truly with thee there is a hidden God: infinite treasure, plentiful redemption: and eternal salvation. The human eye does not see and cannot see: nor any understanding grasp, nor frail reason penetrate; how God is truly entire in this sacrament: is eaten, and yet always remains whole. O what great wonders God works in the sacrament: to Whom naught is impossible to do whatever He will in Heaven and on earth: for the glory and everlasting memorial of His holy name. O saving Victim which openest the gate of Heaven: what wonderful things are said of thee, how unspeakable are all that lie hid in thee: how piously and truly they are believed of thee, and invisibly wrought through thee. These things are proposed to us to be faithfully believed, reverently celebrated: lovingly received, sweetly tasted: incessantly worshipped, ardently embraced: and daily for the salvation of all most pleasingly offered to God the Father. For as often as Mass is celebrated, and the Host consecrated by the word of God: so often does our God come to men: for men come down from Heaven: with men desire to remain, whom He created and redeemed: and intends to make happy for ever as He promised saying: "Behold I am with you all days: even to the consummation of the world." O comforting word, O pious and faithful testament: O great and indubitable and divine promise: to have God ever with him present in the sacrament: Whom the angels have and worship reigning in Heaven.

When therefore the sacred Host at the altar is raised by the hands of the priest and showed to men to be adored: then Christ Who suffered and was crucified for us is presented under a mystic veil: is truly worshipped, devoutly invoked, meekly honoured. Whoever therefore wishes to enter the temple of God, and pray: or recite, or sing, or hear Mass, or celebrate: should first prepare himself, and with a pious intention so dispose himself and consider: as if he were about to go to the Pope and Emperor, to make some petition for himself and his friends in some case of necessity. For it aids him who prays and chants in every place and time: to think of God as present and with the holy angels looking upon him attentively with all-seeing eyes. And as a man prepares himself before prayer: so frequently he finds himself afterwards in prayer. The wanderer prays wanderingly: the frivolous man sings frivolously. Heed, frail man, the reverence due to God: and with holy David go over into the place of the wonderful tabernacle in holy fear: presume not of thyself, but with the publican seek mercy and pardon in the present exile; that hereafter with Lazarus thou mayest merit to have eternal rest and glory in Heaven. Which may Jesus Christ deign to grant us all, the Son of God born of the Virgin Mary: crucified and sacrificed for us: Who with the Father and the Holy Ghost liveth and reigneth God: for ever and ever. Amen.

Here end the Sermons to the Novices.

Here follow certain examples, for the sake of edification.

AN EXAMPLE

A certain religious brother of our house intending to celebrate Mass: first out of charity visited another brother who was seriously ill. The sick man therefore asked him faithfully to pray to the Lord for him in the Mass: and if it pleased the Lord that he might become well again. Then the priest moved with pity, very affectionately and earnestly desiring to fulfil the work of charity: prayed the loving Lord for the health of the brother. And when Mass was over, he at once went to the sick man again: and asked how it was with him. The sick man answered: "Thanks be to God, I feel myself much better by virtue of the Mass, which out of charity you have said for me to-day." After a few days that sick brother regained his health: and making much progress in devotion in holy religion and cheerfully reading devout books and the discourses of the saints: by the ordinance of God he was finally after a few years elected to the priorship.

ANOTHER

A certain ancient brother in our convent was once tormented with excessive pains in the stomach: so that he could neither sit nor sleep quietly for the suffering which he endured within. And when for a whole night and almost to midday he had been so afflicted, and had sought relief by now lying, now rising, and found no remedy: there came to him a certain devout laic to visit him: and compassionating him he said in comfort: "Get up and come with me to the fire: I hope it will do you good as I also have experienced in myself and in others troubled with this pain." The brother at once consented to his advice: and went down from the dormitory with the pains still unrelieved. Coming therefore to the door of the choir he opened the door: desiring to call upon the help of the Lord. He entered the choir therefore: and knelt down before the high altar on the kneeler in presence of the Sacrament. And when he had commenced to pray in the sight of the Lord and before the holy relics enclosed on the altar: the pain gradually ceased. And taking courage he prayed the more until all the pain had ceased. Then rising he gave thanks to God and to His saints and to St. Pantaleon the martyr of Christ: whose feast it then was and whom he loved with a sincere heart. Afterwards with joy of mind going round the altar and devoutly kissing the door of the Sacrament, he went down to the other altars set in the Church, praying and giving thanks and he recovered so far: that he was able the same day to go with the brethren to labour and to the choir.

ANOTHER

A lay servant in a certain house of our Order went to the Church for the sake of devotion to pray: but by the temptation of the devil and overcome by sloth he commenced to sleep there. And when he was lying back to rest: he saw in a dream a venerable Lady standing over him: and saying these words: "If thou wilt sleep: rise from this and go to thy bed. For this place was not made for sleeping: but for watching and praying therein." And he terrified by the vision at once arose: and acknowledging himself guilty narrated these things to others as a warning of correction that they should not sleep in the house of prayer.

ANOTHER

A certain poor woman loving the things that are of God, used frequently to visit the Church: and willingly heard the word of God preached. One day coming from the Church: she was asked what good she had retained of the sermon. And answering briefly she said: "I cannot tell you much: but I have heard this well and retained it, that I do not wish to sin any more." Well and prudently she answered: who took with her the fruit of a good sermon, not to sin any more. Whence Our Saviour in the gospel said to the devout woman: "Blessed are they who hear the word of God: and keep it."

Here end the Sermons to the Novices Regular.

Made in the USA
Las Vegas, NV
29 March 2025

20285045R00105